AF695314

EXPLORING THE IMPACT AND OPPORTUNITIES OF CARBON PRICING IN THE TRANSPORT SECTOR IN CAREC COUNTRIES

JULY 2026

25 CAREC
Central Asia Regional Economic Cooperation

ADB

6 ADB Avenue, Mandaluyong City, 1550 Metro Manila, Philippines
Tel +63 2 8632 4444; Fax +63 2 8636 2444
www.adb.org

ISBN 978-92-9277-866-8 (print); 978-92-9277-867-5 (PDF); 978-92-9277-868-2 (ebook)
Publication Stock No. TCS260282-2
DOI: http://dx.doi.org/10.22617/TCS260282-2

Notes:
In this publication, "$" refers to United States dollars, unless otherwise stated.
ADB recognizes "China" as the People's Republic of China, "Korea" as the Republic of Korea, and "Kyrgyzstan" as the Kyrgyz Republic.

Cover design by Mike Cortes.

CONTENTS

Tables, Figures, and Boxes ... iv
Abbreviations ... vi
Executive Summary ... vii

Chapter 1 | Background ... 1

Chapter 2 | Status: CAREC Countries with Carbon Pricing Instruments ... 2
2.1. Azerbaijan ... 2
2.2. People's Republic of China ... 3
2.3. Georgia ... 4
2.4. Kazakhstan ... 5
2.5. Kyrgyz Republic ... 6
2.6. Mongolia ... 7
2.7. Pakistan ... 9
2.8. Tajikistan ... 10
2.9. Turkmenistan ... 10
2.10. Uzbekistan ... 11
2.11. Conclusions on Carbon Pricing in CAREC Countries ... 11

Chapter 3 | GHG Emission Reduction Options in the Transport Sector ... 13
3.1. GHG Mitigation Options ... 13
3.2. Overview of Transport Measures in CAREC Countries ... 20

Chapter 4 | Carbon Taxes ... 25
4.1. Carbon Tax Instrument ... 25
4.2. Carbon Tax in Transportation—CAREC Countries ... 28
4.3. Opportunities in CAREC Countries ... 31

Chapter 5 | Emissions Trading Systems ... 36
5.1. Emissions Trading System Instrument ... 36
5.2. The Transport Sector and Emissions Trading Systems ... 39
5.3. Opportunities in CAREC Countries ... 43

Chapter 6 | Carbon Markets ... 44
6.1. Carbon Market Overview ... 44
6.2. Carbon Market Transport Projects ... 54
6.3. Options for CAREC Countries ... 63

TABLES, FIGURES, AND BOXES

Tables

1 Overview of Carbon Finance in CAREC Countries 11
2 Overview of Planned Transport Mitigation Measures for CAREC Countries, as of end-2025 24
3 Implicit Carbon Tax on Gasoline Fuels in CAREC Countries, 2024 29
4 Implicit Carbon Tax on Diesel Fuels in CAREC Countries, mid-2024 30
5 Annual Projected Revenue of a Climate Cent Fund per Country 33
6 Potential Annual Transport Emissions Reductions from a Climate Cent Fund 34
7 Registered CDM Transport Projects, as of end-2025 57
8 Active Verified Carbon Standard Transport Projects, end-2025 57
9 Active Gold Standard Transport Projects, end-2025 58
10 Bilateral Article 6.2 Agreements and Projects with CAREC Countries, end-2025 59
11 Article 6.2 Transport Projects, end-2025 60
12 Prior Consideration for Article 6.4 Projects in CAREC Countries, November 2025 61
13 Carbon Markets and Transport Projects 61
14 Transport Project Types Versus Critical Criteria for Carbon Market Projects 62
15 Azerbaijan's Estimated Greenhouse Gas Emissions Reduction Impact per Vehicle Category per Annum 64
16 Estimated Greenhouse Gas Reduction Impact per Vehicle Category per Annum for Georgia 68
17 Estimated Greenhouse Gas Emissions Reduction Impact per Vehicle Category per Annum for Kazakhstan 69
18 Estimated Greenhouse Gas Emissions Reduction Impact per Vehicle Category per Annum for the Kyrgyz Republic 71
19 Estimated Greenhouse Gas Emissions Reduction Impact per Vehicle Category per Annum for Mongolia 72
20 Estimated GHG Emissions Reduction Impact per Vehicle Category per Annum for Pakistan 75
21 Estimated GHG Emissions Reduction Impact per Vehicle Category per Annum for Tajikistan 76
22 Estimated GHG Emissions Reduction Impact per Vehicle Category per Annum for Turkmenistan 77
23 Estimated Greenhouse Gas Emissions Reduction Impact per Vehicle Category per Annum for Uzbekistan 78
24 Matching Priority Areas with Carbon Market Projects per Country 79

Figures

1 Mongolian Domestic Carbon Market Management Structure 8
2 Carbon Tax per Country, 1 April 2025 27
3 Gasoline Explicit Subsidy or Tax in CAREC Countries, 2024 28
4 Diesel Explicit Subsidy or Tax in CAREC Countries, 2024 29
5 Emissions Trading Systems Compliance Price per Country/Region, 1 April 2025 38
6 Tesla's Regulatory Credits Revenue 41
7 Tesla's Regulatory Credits to Total Revenue Ratio 42
8 Tesla's Regulatory Credits per Car 42
9 Process Flow of a Carbon Credit Project 45
10 Volumes and Prices of Voluntary Carbon Markets, 2020–2024 48

Boxes

1 Uzbekistan iCRAFT Project 17
2 Singapore Carbon Tax 26
3 Thai National Voluntary Carbon Market 46
4 South Africa's Carbon Credit Market 47
5 Overview of the Carbon Offsetting and Reduction Scheme for International Aviation 50
6 Overview of the Paris Agreement 51
7 Thai–Swiss e-Bus Project 52
8 Japan Joint Crediting Mechanism 60

ABBREVIATIONS

ADB	Asian Development Bank
BAU	business-as-usual
BRT	bus rapid transit
CAREC	Central Asia Regional Economic Cooperation Program
CCER	China Certified Emission Reduction
CDM	Clean Development Mechanism
PRC	People's Republic of China
CNG	compressed natural gas
CORSIA	Carbon Offsetting and Reduction Scheme for International Aviation
ETS	emissions trading system
EU	European Union
EV	electric vehicle
GHG	greenhouse gas
HSR	high-speed rail
ICE	internal combustion engine
IFI	international financial institution
IMO	International Marine Organization
ITMO	internationally transferred mitigation outcome
ITMS	Intelligent Traffic Management Systems
JCM	Joint Crediting Mechanism
LRT	light-rail transit
LUCF	land-use change and forestry
MRV	monitoring, reporting, and verification
NDC	nationally determined contribution
NMT	nonmotorized transport
PACM	Paris Agreement Crediting Mechanism
UNDP	United Nations Development Programme
UNFCCC	United Nations Framework Convention on Climate Change
VCS	Verified Carbon Standard
ZEV	zero-emission vehicle

WEIGHTS AND MEASURES

CO_2	carbon dioxide
gCO_2/km	grams of CO_2 per kilometer
$GtCO_2$	gigatons of CO_2
km	kilometer
L	liter
$MtCO_2$	million tons of CO_2
tCO_2	tons of carbon dioxide
tCO_2e	tons of carbon dioxide equivalent
t-km	ton-kilometer

EXECUTIVE SUMMARY

The transport sector is one of the world's largest contributors to greenhouse gas (GHG) emissions. Carbon pricing, including mechanisms like carbon taxes and emissions trading systems (ETS), is emerging as a powerful tool to incentivize emissions reductions, drive technological innovation, and promote sustainable practices. This study aims to evaluate global and regional trends in carbon pricing in the transport sector and to identify carbon pricing opportunities in the Central Asia Regional Economic Cooperation (CAREC) Program. The report assesses global trends and policies in carbon pricing mechanisms and their application in the transport sector, analyzes the status of CAREC countries in carbon pricing mechanisms, and develops a potential pipeline of projects for the CAREC region. These projects can create revenue streams for governments, which can then be reinvested into low-carbon mobility and improve the financial viability of low-carbon transport measures.

The contribution of transport emissions, excluding land-use change and forestry, to total GHG emissions in CAREC countries ranges from 5% for Mongolia to 23% for Georgia, with a median of 9% for all CAREC countries. Transport emissions in all CAREC countries are growing significantly faster than overall GHG emissions, showing the importance of introducing effective measures to curb these emissions.

The main measures identified by CAREC countries to reduce GHG transport emissions relate to electric mobility, low-carbon fuels, expansion and improvement of public transport services, nonmotorized transport, efficiency improvements in the transport sector, and shifting road to rail and road to shipping for both freight and passenger transport. Carbon pricing instruments for transport have been included by the People's Republic of China (PRC) in their subnational ETS. CAREC countries show that the transport sector can play a role in carbon markets.

Carbon pricing is an instrument that captures the external costs of GHG emissions, giving economic actors a pricing signal. Carbon pricing instruments are primarily carbon taxes, ETS, and carbon crediting mechanisms.

Carbon taxes have been imposed in numerous countries worldwide for over 3 decades, with pricing levels ranging from \$0.10 to \$150 per ton of carbon dioxide (tCO_2). Research has shown that carbon taxes have a larger impact on fuels used in the transport and housing sectors than in other economic sectors as the production of goods or services in these sectors cannot be reallocated across borders. Some countries allow for offsetting of carbon taxes with carbon credits. Within CAREC countries, no country has a carbon tax, but Azerbaijan, Mongolia, and Tajikistan are considering establishing one.

Most CAREC countries have a tax on transport fuels, which can be expressed as an implicit carbon tax (i.e., a tax embedded in fuel prices through an existing value-added, excise, or other tax, rather than a direct tax, which is related to the carbon dioxide [CO_2] emissions of the fuel). The value in 2024 ranged from $4–$100 per tCO_2 for diesel and $4–$145 per tCO_2 for gasoline. Azerbaijan, Kazakhstan, and Turkmenistan sell transport fuels (gasoline and diesel) significantly below costs.

Transport fuel taxes are ineffective in significantly influencing demand in the short term because fuel demand at any given point in time is inelastic. Hence fuel price increases, e.g., via a carbon tax, are a poor short-term tool for achieving GHG emissions reductions.

Significant revenue streams for governments can arise from a CO_2 tax on fuels. Such revenue streams can form part of the general budget and be used to reduce other taxes, they can be returned to the population or companies, or they can be earmarked for specific purposes, such as road construction or GHG mitigation projects. If carbon tax revenues finance GHG mitigation projects the impact is twofold: a reduction of fuel consumption due to the carbon tax and related fuel price increase, plus a reduction in GHG emissions due to investments in GHG mitigation projects. Based on prevailing prices for high-quality carbon projects in the transport sector, the indirect impact from investments of a carbon tax revenue on GHG mitigation projects is estimated to be 50–100 times larger than the direct impact resulting from reduced fuel consumption. This means that a low-carbon tax can be established while still achieving a high GHG emissions reduction impact if revenues are recycled to investments in GHG mitigation projects.

A low-carbon tax of $0.01 per liter of gasoline and diesel sold, for instance (a "climate cent fund"), could be used to create a steady revenue stream for a fund, which then purchases domestic carbon reductions from the transport sector. A small increase in the fuel price directly will not result in significant emissions reductions due to the price inelasticity of fuel. The estimated emissions reductions are a consequence of using proceeds from the increase to pay for transport mitigation activities, e.g., through a carbon market system. Such a fund could achieve, on average, 75% of the estimated domestic unconditional nationally determined contribution (NDC) target for transport sectors in CAREC countries listed in their climate action plans under the Paris Agreement. Surplus reductions could be sold, together with corresponding adjustments to other countries, allowing for further growth of the fund and additional transport mitigation measures.

An ETS under a cap-and-trade system is managed by a governing jurisdiction that sets a limit (cap) on total emissions for obligated participants covered by the ETS within a given period. An ETS under a baseline-and-credit system sets emissions targets (which are also caps) for regulated entities, which can then earn tradable credits for emissions below their baseline. Allowances can be traded among market participants. ETS can be implemented on a regional, national, or subnational level. Numerous countries or subnational entities have already implemented ETS, with the price rate varying from $1 to $70 per tCO_2. An ETS in general only includes certain sectors (typically the energy and industry sectors) and large emitters. Most ETS allow for quantitatively limited offsets with carbon credits from non-ETS entities. ETS for the transport sector are considered to have the largest potential in relation to establishing fuel efficiency, CO_2 standards, or targets for new vehicles registered in a given country, combined with tradable permits.

Within CAREC countries, the PRC has established multiple subnational ETS and a national ETS, which was structured based on the experiences in subnational pilot schemes. Some subnational ETS included the transport sector. Kazakhstan implemented an ETS in 2013 with regulated entities from the industry, energy, and mining sectors. Offsets generated by domestic projects can be used to meet compliance obligations within the ETS; however, the current price of around $1/t$CO_2$ is not attractive enough to develop a transport offset project. Azerbaijan, Pakistan, and Tajikistan are considering establishing ETS.

A transport sector can be integrated into an ETS by (i) including large transport companies as regulated entities, (ii) including transport fuels in an ETS, or (iii) establishing an allowance system for CO_2 emissions of vehicles.

California's cap-and-trade system includes fuel distributors. They can invest in low-carbon fuels, e.g., by blending biofuels with fossil fuels, to reduce the number of allowances they need to acquire.

Multiple countries, including the PRC, have established CO_2 emissions targets or standards for vehicles combined with tradable zero-emission vehicle credits or with pooling of manufacturers. Such emission or regulatory credits can in general be averaged across a company's fleets, banked for future years, or traded with other manufacturers. Common points of such an approach are (i) the setting of an ambitious and clear grams of CO_2 per kilometer standard per newly registered vehicle based on a standardized test procedure; (ii) a high noncompliance penalty to spur sale, production, and/or import of low-carbon vehicles; and (iii) a mechanism that allows for trading or pooling to increase system efficiency. Emission pooling or trading significantly impacts electric vehicle (EV) sales by creating financial incentives for car manufacturers to increase EV production and sales. Tesla, for example, had regulatory revenues due to regulatory credits of initially close to $4,000 (2016) then $1,500 (2024) per EV sold. This approach applies the polluter pays principle, requires no fiscal resources from governments, leaves freedom to choose to customers, and is an effective means to achieve significant GHG reductions of the transport sector in a technology-neutral manner. CAREC countries mostly use European Union vehicle emission standards for pollutants, which could be linked with CO_2 vehicle emission standards. As most CAREC countries have either no or a limited vehicle industry, an ETS with tradable permits for CO_2 vehicle emissions would need to be tied to vehicle importers and dealers (Switzerland for example uses this approach).

Carbon markets are systems wherein carbon credits issued for activities that reduce or remove GHG emissions are traded. Basically, there are (i) national compliance markets created through laws and regulations by regional or national governments or international compliance markets; and (ii) voluntary carbon markets on a regional, national, and international scale. In voluntary markets, participants have no formal obligations and set their own goals to meet voluntary commitments while in compliance markets the goals are established by governments or international treaties.

All CAREC countries are in principle interested in participating in carbon markets. The PRC was the largest supplier of carbon credit projects under the Clean Development Mechanism (CDM) developed under the Kyoto Protocol, and has established various subregional markets as well as a national carbon market. Georgia, Kazakhstan, the Kyrgyz Republic, Mongolia, and Uzbekistan have signed bilateral agreements under Article 6.2 of the Paris Agreement with either Japan, the Republic of Korea and/or Switzerland, though no transport projects are yet under development. Various CAREC countries have also participated in voluntary carbon projects, though not involving the transport sector. Uzbekistan has a pilot policy crediting project supported by the World Bank, though it is not linked to the transport sector.

Domestic carbon markets have been established in more than 30 countries at national or subnational levels, mostly in conjunction with an ETS, where offsets can be used at least partially instead of allowances, or in systems with a carbon or environmental tax, where carbon credits can be used. International compliance markets include those established previously under the CDM, the new international compliance market under Articles 6.2 and 6.4 of the Paris Agreement, and the Carbon Offsetting and Reduction Scheme for International Aviation (CORSIA) managed by the International Civil Aviation Organization.

Carbon credit prices are subject to very high price volatility. Prices paid in the voluntary carbon markets depend on project type, with average reported prices in 2024 of $\$6/tCO_{2.}$ International compliance markets (the Paris Agreement crediting mechanism and CORSIA) reported prices in mid-2025 of $\$25/tCO_2$ to $\$50/tCO_2$. These prices are expected to increase. Domestic market prices paid depend on the country, with prices ranging from less than $\$1/tCO_2$ to over $\$200/tCO_{2}$.

The most promising transport project types for carbon markets in terms of potential GHG reduction magnitude and the availability of internationally approved methodologies are electric mobility projects, urban public transport projects, and rail projects. The most appropriate are electric mobility projects; public transport and rail projects often suffer from very long gestation periods and the involvement of public actors using difficult decision-making processes. These projects are often more appropriate for other forms of climate finance, e.g., as offered by the Green Climate Fund. Electric mobility has the potential to achieve significant emissions reductions in the transport sector while also contributing to sustainable development through reduced air pollutants. This creates business opportunities for CAREC countries.

It is recommended that countries build a pipeline of transport projects for national or international carbon markets, especially in the areas of electric mobility, urban public transport, and rail, thereby contributing toward achievement of the conditional and unconditional targets as defined in countries' NDCs.

Chapter 1

BACKGROUND

The transport sector is one of the largest contributors to greenhouse gas (GHG) emissions globally. Carbon pricing is emerging as a powerful tool to incentivize emissions reductions, drive technological innovation, and promote sustainable transport. Carbon pricing is defined by the World Bank as "an instrument that captures the external costs of GHG emissions and ties them to their sources through a price, usually in the form of a price on the carbon dioxide (CO_2) emitted."[1] This gives economic actors a pricing signal and incentivizes GHG reductions in financial terms. Carbon pricing instruments are primarily carbon taxes, emissions trading systems (ETS), and carbon crediting mechanisms.

This study aims to evaluate trends in carbon pricing in transport, assess its economic and operational impacts, and identify business and policy opportunities created by its implementation in the Central Asia Regional Economic Cooperation (CAREC) Program, a partnership of 11 countries (Afghanistan, Azerbaijan, the People's Republic of China (PRC), Georgia, Kazakhstan, the Kyrgyz Republic, Mongolia, Pakistan, Tajikistan, Turkmenistan, and Uzbekistan), with the Asian Development Bank (ADB) acting as its Secretariat. This report covers all CAREC countries except for Afghanistan.[2] The findings will inform policymakers, government, transport operators, and private sector stakeholders on strategies to utilize carbon pricing mechanisms while capitalizing on emerging opportunities in the CAREC region.

The approach within each section is to discuss a carbon pricing instrument, examine its general application to the transport sector, then review its application and potential in CAREC countries.

1 World Bank Group. Carbon Pricing.

2 ADB placed its regular assistance to Afghanistan on hold effective 15 August 2021.

Chapter 2

STATUS: CAREC COUNTRIES WITH CARBON PRICING INSTRUMENTS

2.1. Azerbaijan

Azerbaijan is exploring the implementation of various carbon pricing instruments. Its Ministry of Economy is considering two primary options: the introduction of a carbon tax or of a domestic carbon market/ETS.[3] The EU4Climate program is supporting Azerbaijan in its preparation to develop a carbon market and establish a new carbon markets unit in the relevant ministries.[4]

As of the end of 2025, Azerbaijan has no formal carbon taxation framework. The World Bank has suggested that the government introduce an upstream carbon tax, which would be levied on the carbon content of all fuels, whether imported or domestically produced, at the point they enter the economy. The tax could cover nearly 60% of all generated emissions and the current excise tax framework could be adapted or extended to accommodate the carbon tax collection.[5]

Another World Bank modeling exercise considered different policy options to employ to meet Azerbaijan's nationally determined contributions (NDCs) under the Paris Agreement.[6] It suggested that the best option is the combination of a fossil fuel tax policy removal, which includes the elimination of subsidies for fossil fuels along with a gradual introduction of carbon pricing. The model indicates that eliminating two-thirds of current fossil fuel subsidies is sufficient to achieve the targets for 2030. Additionally, the model considers that the revenue generated by carbon pricing should be redistributed to households, and a reduction in factor taxes (capital, labor, land) should also be considered. Transport sector emissions reductions could be achieved through a combination of mode shift and the introduction of clean fuels and energy efficiency measures, with the rail sector expected to play a bigger role. By 2060, conventional fossil fuels would be phased out.[7]

Another economic modeling and analysis explored potential scenarios involving carbon prices as a proxy for efficient decarbonization policies, alongside the gradual phase-out of natural gas and oil subsidies, to meet NDCs. Achieving the 2030 NDC target could involve carbon prices reaching \$25 per ton of CO_2 (tCO_2) (footnote 6) in 2035, \$41/tCO_2 by 2050, and \$62/tCO_2 in 2060, while a net-zero scenario by 2060 might see prices increase to \$30/tCO_2 in 2035 and \$280/tCO_2 in 2060.

3 K. Sadigov. 2024. Azerbaijan Eyes Implementing Carbon Tax or Emissions Trading System. *Report News Agency*. 6 November.
4 EU4Climate. 2023. *Enabling Ambitious Climate Action*. Eastern Partnership.
5 K. Gasimov. 2025. WB Recommends Azerbaijan to Start Carbon Pricing with Carbon Tax. *Report News Agency*. 30 May.
6 World Bank Group. 2023. *Country Climate and Development Report for Azerbaijan*.
7 World Bank Group. 2023. *Country Climate and Development Report for Azerbaijan*. p.28.

Azerbaijan has registered various projects under the Clean Development Mechanism (CDM) developed under the Kyoto Protocol, though none from the transport sector. It has also requested the registration of a hydropower project under the Global Carbon Council standard. Azerbaijan and Japan signed a memorandum of cooperation in 2022 through the Joint Crediting Mechanism (JCM), though no projects have yet been proposed or implemented.

2.2. People's Republic of China

The PRC does not have a national CO_2 tax. Its Environmental Protection Tax (2018) applies to conventional pollutants but excludes CO_2. A carbon tax proposed in 2010–2012 by the Ministry of Finance was never enacted.

The PRC has various subnational pilot ETS and a national ETS. Beijing, Guangdong, Shanghai, Shenzhen, and Tianjin have each run pilot ETS since 2013, while Chongqing and Hubei began pilot ETS in 2014, and Fujian started one in 2016.[8] Cities with ETS that cover transport include Beijing (public transport), Fujian (aviation), Guangdong (aviation), Shanghai (maritime shipping, road transport, and aviation), and Shenzhen (urban buses and taxis).

The national ETS started implementation in 2021 has the following main features:

- **Legal basis.** Interim Regulations on the Administration of Carbon Emissions Trading (State Council, effective 1 May 2024).
- **Coverage (2025).** Power since 2021, with steel, cement, and aluminium added in 2025 for 2024 emissions, including tetrafluoromethane and hexafluoroethane, both potent perfluorocarbon GHGs, primarily emitted during aluminum smelting and semiconductor manufacturing and significantly contributing to climate change.
- **Threshold.** The ETS covers facilities producing greater than 26,000 tCO_2 equivalent (tCO_2e)/year in covered sectors.
- **Offsets.** China Certified Emission Reduction (CCER) credits of up to 5% of verified emissions are offered. The original CCER system was suspended in 2017, reactivated in 2021, and relaunched as CCER 2.0 in 2024, with a new registry effective from January 2025.
- **Allocation:** Allocation is based on free, output-based benchmarks, with auctioning foreseen in future.
- **Prices.** In 2024 prices average $13.50 per tCO_2; prices have more than doubled since 2021 and reached $14 in late 2024.
- **Market size.** The market size was originally around 40% of national CO_2, with expansion to new sectors boosting coverage to around 60%, or around 8 gigatons of CO_2 ($GtCO_2$). Around 1,500 new firms have been added.
- **Compliance.** Monitoring, reporting, verification, and penalties increased in 2024.

8 World Bank Group. State and Trends of Carbon Pricing Dashboard (accessed 27 April 2026).

- **Future.** Absolute caps in some industries are expected by 2027, with broader absolute caps and auctioning by 2030. New sectors under discussion include chemicals, papermaking, and domestic aviation.

Major challenges faced by the ETS include a generous free allocation of allowances, resulting in low carbon prices and limited incentives to reduce emissions. This is however typical for the start of an ETS and can be related to political buy-in to the system and a temporary challenge. Implementation of the ETS continues to evolve, with ongoing efforts to harmonize monitoring, reporting, and verification practices across regions. The PRC's ETC offers many insights as it has incorporated various pilot ETS in different areas of the transport sector.

In 2012, the PRC launched the GHG Voluntary Emission Reduction Program with more than 1,000 registered projects, and companies and civil actors able to buy and sell voluntary credits. The market was relaunched in 2024 as CCER 2.0. Some CCER credits are eligible as offsets under the ETS (with a limit of 5%). The initial CCER 2.0 transactions in 2024 saw state-owned enterprises (e.g., China National Offshore Oil Corporation) buying credits, with volatile prices ranging from $0.40 to $25/tCO_2$. As of the end of 2025, there is no provision for transport projects under the CCER 2.0.

2.3. Georgia

The carbon market in Georgia is still in its early stages of development. At the national level, neither a carbon tax nor an ETS has been introduced. Instead, the government has focused on establishing fundamental infrastructure, such as a national monitoring, reporting, and verification (MRV) system for emissions, as well as cooperation within international carbon trading mechanisms.[9]

In September 2024, the Government of Georgia approved amendments to the Environmental Protection Act, introducing an MRV system for GHG emissions. Under the adopted regulations, from 1 January 2026, certain industrial and aviation companies will be required to obtain a GHG emissions permit, for which they will need to prepare an emissions monitoring plan and report regularly to an authorized body.[10] A national emissions accounting infrastructure is being established; all major emitters will measure and verify their emissions, which is necessary for the launch of market mechanisms and accurate tracking of progress. Thus, between 2024 and 2026, the legal framework for the functioning of the carbon market in Georgia and participation in international emissions trading will be established. Overall, Georgia's regulatory and strategic framework is increasingly aligned with European Union (EU) policies under the Association Agreement. The European Commission's 2023 report notes that Georgia has adopted a climate change strategy and action plan for 2030. However, overall alignment with the EU acquis in the climate field is still at an early stage.[11]

9 European Commission. 2024. Commission Staff Working Document. Georgia 2024 Report. Accompanying the document: Communication from the Commission to the European Parliament, the Council, the European Economic and Social Committee and the Committee of the Regions. p. 86.

10 Government of Georgia, Ministry of Environmental Protection and Agriculture. 2024. Amendments were Made to the Law of Georgia on Environmental Protection. News release. 16 September.

11 The EU acquis in climate refers to the comprehensive collection of EU laws, regulations, and binding targets designed to combat climate change.

Georgia does not have a national carbon market and no sector-specific cap-and-trade programs are in place. The creation of a domestic ETS is seen as a long-term task requiring sufficient emissions for effective trading and the development of institutional experience. In its 2021 NDC, Georgia explicitly stated that it seeks participation in international and voluntary carbon markets, including under Article 6 of the Paris Agreement, as one of the tools for achieving its goals. Accordingly, the country is focusing on cross-border carbon trading mechanisms rather than on creating an isolated domestic market. Georgia has concluded its first bilateral agreements under Article 6 of the Paris Agreement with Switzerland and Japan.

2.4. Kazakhstan

Kazakhstan is a party to the Paris Agreement and an active participant in climate initiatives in Central Asia at both national and international levels. In recent years, the country has adopted a comprehensive legal framework and developed a strategy to achieve carbon neutrality by 2060. Kazakhstan holds a leading position in the region in implementing ETS and developing voluntary carbon markets.

Since 2013, Kazakhstan has operated an ETS that allows domestic enterprises to accumulate carbon credits and participate in international markets.[12] The legal basis is set in the Environmental Code of Kazakhstan—a state legislative act that mandates participation in the ETS for specific sectors. JSC Jasyl Damu (Green Development), under the Ministry of Ecology and Natural Resources, manages the ETS. Facilities exceeding an emissions threshold of 20,000 tCO_2/year must participate in the ETS. As of the end of 2025, the ETS includes 135 companies from the energy, mining, and industry sectors, with 212 installations representing about half of all GHG emissions, with projects underway to expand sector coverage. The transport sector in Kazakhstan, as of the end of 2025, is not included in the ETS and is not subject to a mandatory carbon tax. Allowances are allocated for free, which limits the market and keeps the price at around \$1/tCO_2. Offsets generated by domestic projects (GHG reduction or absorption activities) in all economic sectors outside the scope of the ETS can be used to meet compliance obligations. There are no quantitative limits, meaning 100% of emissions can be covered using offset credits. In its NDC 3.0, Kazakhstan announced the intention to strengthen its ETS with tighter carbon budgets and improved MRV, enabling it to participate in Article 6 of the Paris Agreement (explained in National Carbon Market Section) with clear authorizations and corresponding adjustments.[13] Since 2022, the ETS has undergone reform to increase transparency and improve its MRV system. ADB developed a comprehensive set of recommendations on MRV processes related to Kazakhstan's ETS, including a road map for implementation to guide the government on short- and long-term priorities.[14] An expansion

[12] Astana International Financial Center. 2025. *Emissions Trading Systems and Voluntary Carbon Market: Global Overview and Prospects for Kazakhstan*.

[13] Government of Kazakhstan. 2025. *Nationally Determined Contribution of the Republic of Kazakhstan to the Global Response to Climate Change Until 2035*.

[14] ADB. 2024. Regional: Supporting the Implementation of ADB's Climate Change Operational Framework 2017–2030 - Establishing Mechanisms to Measure, Monitor, and Report on Commitments made under the Paris Agreement (Subproject 3). Kazakhstan: Support for the Enhancement of the Monitoring, Review, and Verification System. Consultant's report (TA 9720-REG).

of the ETS is planned for 2025–2030, including integrating the transport sector. The possibility of introducing a parallel carbon tax is also being considered. The ETS will be integrated with international markets, including through participation in the Global Carbon Pricing Challenge and projects under Article 6 of the Paris Agreement. The Ministry of Ecology and Natural Resources of Kazakhstan, together with Jasyl Damu and with World Bank support, is implementing a project to improve and further develop the ETS, including through digitalization, auction-based trading, and market expansion to new sectors.

In 2023, a national voluntary carbon credit trading platform was launched at the Astana International Financial Center. The center acts as a catalyst and coordinator for the development of sustainable finance markets in Kazakhstan. An integration with VERRA and the Gold Standard ensures international recognition of offset projects. Issuance of up to 43 million voluntary carbon credits is planned by 2030 from projects in agriculture, energy efficiency, and forestry. However, it is unclear who should purchase such credits and if, at as of the end of 2025 ETS prices, this is a valid business proposition for project owners. Kazakhstan has also signed bilateral Article 6.2 agreements with Japan and the Republic of Korea.

2.5. Kyrgyz Republic

Although the Kyrgyz Republic plans to achieve carbon neutrality by 2050, as of the end of 2025 it does not have an explicit carbon pricing instrument such as a carbon tax or ETS, although fuel excise taxes provide an implicit carbon price. There is no operational carbon pricing instrument in place, but its legal and institutional framework is evolving, including through draft climate legislation and institutions supporting climate finance and carbon market cooperation. In July 2023, Japan and the Kyrgyz Republic signed a memorandum of cooperation to establish the JCM. A Project Idea Note (initial project document) for the modernization of boiler houses was approved. On 13 November 2023, the Kyrgyz Stock Exchange signed an agreement with LLC DiG to create a market for trading CO_2 emissions allowances and to develop voluntary carbon credits.[15] As of early 2026, this is an initiative only and the market is not yet fully operational.

The Kyrgyz Republic is in the final stages of developing a comprehensive Climate Action Law designed to establish a unified framework for national climate policy, create an institutional framework for climate actions, and implement effective mechanisms for climate change mitigation and adaptation. The law, developed in collaboration with partners like the United Nations Development Programme (UNDP), is intended to strengthen the country's ability to secure international climate financing, engage in carbon markets, and meet its climate goals under the Paris Agreement. Its goal is to achieve carbon neutrality, adapt to climate change, and create a national system for MRV of climate actions.[16]

15 Kyrgyz Stock Exchange. 2023. The Kyrgyz Stock Exchange and LLC "DiG" Signed the Agreement on Joint Activities on Development of the Market for Trading in Quotas for Greenhouse Gas Emissions. News release. 13 November.

16 Aarhus Centers of Kyrgyzstan. 2025. Public Hearing of the Draft Law of the Kyrgyz Republic "On Climate Activities."

2.6. Mongolia

Mongolia is exploring and planning the implementation of a carbon tax as a key component of its climate action strategy, though a formal system is not yet established. Carbon pricing is seen as a critical tool for incentivizing emissions reductions, while driving investment shifts toward greener alternatives, and promoting sustainable consumption patterns as well. A carbon tax is considered a promising new revenue source for Mongolia's green transition, particularly given its potential to modernize the energy market. The development of domestic carbon pricing in Mongolia as of the end of 2025 is in its initial stages, with a primary focus on building capacity for economic impact modeling related to a carbon tax.[17]

A 2024 policy brief analyzed the potential macroeconomic effects of introducing a carbon tax in Mongolia and found it could positively impact gross domestic product and employment while effectively reducing GHG emissions.[18] The analysis outlined a scenario where a carbon tax would start at $2/tCO_2$ in 2025, then increase by $2 annually until reaching $18 in 2033. From 2034, it would increase by $2.5 annually, reaching $35 by 2040. The proposed carbon tax primarily targets emissions from the energy and industry sectors, which together were responsible for 97% of Mongolia's GHG emissions in 2020. Electricity and heat generation account for over half of the energy sector's emissions. The policy brief also explored how tax revenues could be utilized: (i) 50% would be returned to private households as lump-sum transfers; (ii) 25% would be invested in the expansion of renewable energy sources, and (iii) 25% would be allocated to converting the heating supply, aiming for complete decarbonization by 2050. An upstream carbon tax could be more effective than an ETS due to Mongolia's limited institutional capacity; this scenario considers taxing carbon emissions directly at the source, such as coal mines, oil wells, and importers, and would primarily affect state-owned enterprises.[19]

Within the institutional framework, the Ministry of Finance is responsible for overseeing carbon taxation policies, while a broader domestic carbon pricing framework involves a comprehensive institutional structure that includes the National Climate Committee as the high-level decision-making body, the Ministry of Economy and Development for strategy and policy development, the Mongolian Environment Civil Council for cross-sector coordination and implementation, and the Climate Change Research and Coordination Center for MRV and GHG inventory responsibilities.

A key prerequisite for the effectiveness of a carbon tax in Mongolia is energy price reform in the electricity and heat sectors to ensure that the costs of emissions are passed through to end-users. Also, institutional coordination requires improvement, as does capacity for data collection and monitoring. Mongolia furthermore lacks clear procedures for authorizing projects, defining eligible activities, using internationally transferred mitigation outcomes (ITMOs), and implementing MRV consistent with international requirements.

17 Green Climate Fund. 2025. *Advancing Carbon Market Readiness in Mongolia*.
18 GIZ. 2024. *Policy Brief: Macroeconomic Effects of Carbon Pricing in Mongolia (Macroeconomic Modeling of a Carbon Tax)*.
19 World Bank Group. 2024. *Mongolia—Country Climate and Development Report*.

Mongolia has participated actively in international carbon markets, including 14 projects under the CDM and JCM. Several voluntary schemes have been developed, and there are plans to also engage in transactions under Article 6 of the Paris Agreement. UNDP Mongolia has developed a comprehensive road map for the country's strategic approach to engaging with both voluntary and compliance carbon markets. Bilateral Article 6.2 agreements are in place with Japan, the Republic of Korea, and Singapore. Since 2013, Mongolia and Japan have a bilateral cooperation agreement under the JCM.

Private Mongolian entities like XacBank, Clean Energy Asia LLC, and the Mongolian Society for Range Management have already developed projects that meet voluntary carbon market requirements in sectors such as energy conservation, land use, rangelands, and renewable energy.[20]

Figure 1 shows the initial structure of the Mongolian Domestic Carbon Market operational flow. The National Climate Committee and the Carbon Market Office are the central agencies. Under the project cycle, the committee, office, and Carbon Market Subcommittees handle project registration and carbon credit issuance, while the National Agency of Meteorology and Environmental Monitoring and the Agency for Land Administration and Management, Geodesy, and Cartography handle the monitoring and feed the database for inventory, monitoring, and assessment.

Figure 1: Mongolian Domestic Carbon Market Management Structure

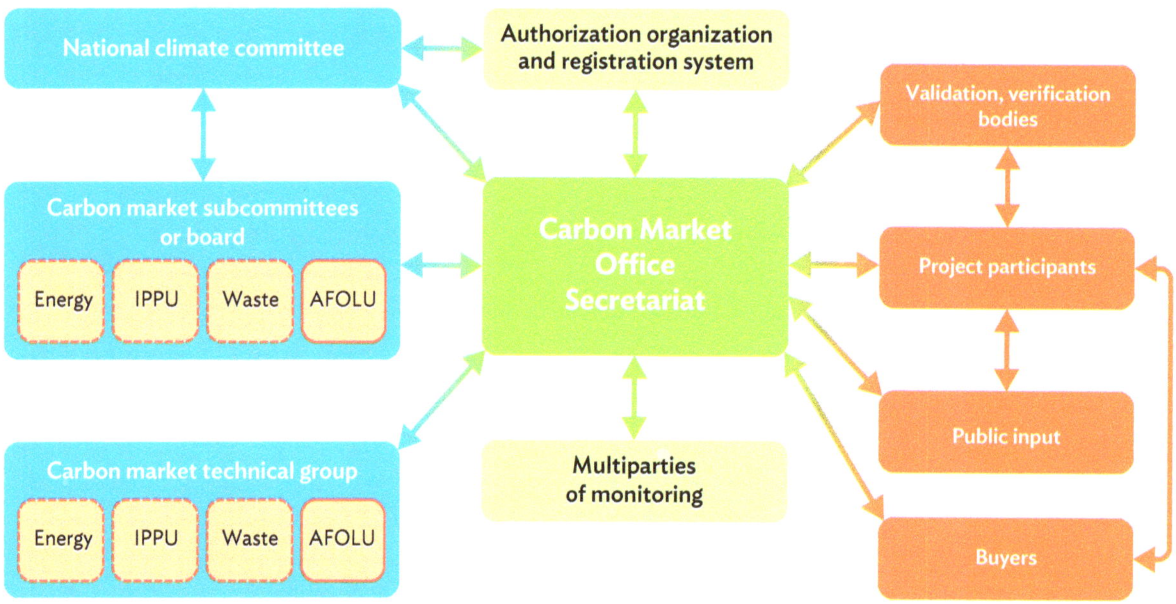

AFOLU = agriculture, forestry, and other land use; IPPU = industrial processes and product use.
Source: S. Enkhtaivan and S. Dolgorsuren. 2024. *Scaling Up Carbon Sequestration in Mongolian Rangelands through a Carbon Crediting and Market Mechanism*. Food and Agricultural Organization of the United Nations and United Nations Development Programme.

[20] Xacbank. 2025. *Annual Report 2024*; Mongolian Society for Range Management. Linking Herders to the Carbon Market Project.

2.7. Pakistan

Pakistan's engagement with carbon market mechanisms dates to 2006, when it began hosting CDM projects under the Kyoto Protocol. As of 2026, Pakistan had granted as host country an approval of 76 CDM project activities, with 37 registered by the CDM executive board, mainly in the energy efficiency and renewable energy sectors.[21]

In 2018, the National Committee on the Establishment of Carbon Markets was established under the Ministry of Climate Change and Environment Coordination to assess the participation of Pakistan in carbon markets, and to review proposed mechanisms and design a domestic ETS framework, including MRV infrastructure.[22] Pakistan's carbon market framework includes guidelines for Article 6.8 and compliance-based activities under Article 6 of the Paris Agreement, with the purpose of attracting green investments and funding mitigation projects locally and internationally. Pakistan is also in the process of formally implementing a national ETS to develop an internal carbon market.

The EU's Carbon Border Adjustment Mechanism, to be fully integrated with the EU ETS by 2026, will impose tariffs on carbon-intensive imports like steel, cement, and aluminum, with textiles (Pakistan's largest export sector) likely included by 2030. Pakistan's electricity sector is approximately 1.44 times more carbon-intensive than the EU average, exposing its exporters to penalties. A domestic carbon price is seen as a strategic measure to help Pakistani exporters comply with the Carbon Border Adjustment Mechanism, avoid tariffs while having to pay potentially lower prices for domestic carbon credits or allowances, and enhance export competitiveness in an increasingly carbon-conscious global market, while avoiding carbon costs on imports of certain carbon-intensive goods.[23]

Pakistan's carbon market framework and the implementation mechanism of the projects will be governed mainly by the Ministry of Climate Change and Environmental Coordination through the Carbon Market Working Group, whose function is to maintain the transparency and integrity of market operations, while the National Carbon Registry develops and supervises the domestic MRV system. The framework includes obligatory fees channeled to Pakistan's Nationally Designated Authority, with 5% of the credits generated in all projects deducted and credited to Pakistan's voluntary NDC adjustments; a corresponding adjustment fee would be applied and calculated at 12% of the net revenue collected from the sale of carbon credits, with half of that revenue channeled to the province where the project is based, and half credited to the Pakistan Climate Change Fund. Additionally, 1% of gross revenues generated from sales would go to the federal government for administrative costs.

[21] Government of Pakistan, Ministry of Climate Change and Environmental Coordination. 2019. *Study on the Introduction of Carbon Pricing Instruments in Pakistan*.

[22] Government of Pakistan, Ministry of Climate Change and Environmental Coordination. 2024. *Pakistan Policy Guidelines for Trading in Carbon Markets*.

[23] A. Q. Suleri. 2025. Our Carbon Bill is Coming Due. *Geo News*. 24 March.

2.8. Tajikistan

While carbon market mechanisms are not yet in place, Tajikistan's policy documents—including the 2023–2037 Green Economy Strategy—already highlight carbon credits and international offset mechanisms under Article 6 of the Paris Agreement as potential tools for financing green projects. The NDC Climate Finance Plan (2022, presented in July 2024) identifies Article 6 carbon markets as one of the key sources of resources. Linking these goals to the Sustainable Development Goals and the national development strategy to 2030, the country aims to align environmental action with economic modernization and job creation.

The Strategy for the Development of Green Economy in the Republic of Tajikistan for 2023–2037 is key for carbon markets and carbon pricing.[24] It aims at transitioning to low-carbon, sustainable development and contains specific targets for reducing GHG emissions by 2030 and by 2050. It envisages implementing measures such as institutional reforms, economic mechanisms (including the development of an ETS and/or carbon tax), and incentives for electric transport to achieve targets.

Tajikistan is discussing plans to introduce a carbon pricing mechanism. It is expected to establish a legal framework for MRV by 2025 and launch the emissions pricing system itself (e.g., tax or trading) by 2030.[25] So far, no official decisions or regulations on the introduction of a carbon tax have been adopted. The government is reportedly considering different options for carbon pricing instruments, but no formal commitments have been made. The national strategy and plans reflect a general course toward a green economy and reduction of GHG emissions, but the specific mechanism of carbon taxation is only at the conceptualization stage. The World Bank and others note that the introduction of a moderate carbon tax could provide additional revenue to the budget and contribute to the achievement of emission reduction targets.[26]

2.9. Turkmenistan

Turkmenistan has no fully-fledged national carbon market yet, but the country is gradually participating in voluntary mechanisms. According to initial projections, the potential volume of voluntary carbon credits issued in Turkmenistan could reach approximately 1.8 million units by 2030. The Ministry of Environmental Protection and the Ministry of Finance and Economy together with UNDP have started preparatory work on the development and implementation of a national MRV system for their NDC.[27] The system should be developed in 2026 and is expected to give a boost to the development of the carbon market.

[24] Government of Tajikistan. 2022. *Strategy for the Development of a Green Economy in the Republic of Tajikistan for 2023–2037*. In Russian.

[25] Asia Plus News. 2024. How Introduction of Carbon Tax can Help Central Asia Reduce Emissions. 12 February.

[26] World Bank. 2024. Tajikistan Country Climate and Development Report.

[27] Regional Environmental Centre for Central Asia. 2024. CACCC [Central Asia Climate Change Conference]-2024: The Climate Work of Turkmenistan in Brief. News release. 4 June.

2.10. Uzbekistan

Uzbekistan's carbon market is at the formation stage, but significant laws and the first steps for its launch and initial financing have been adopted. In 2023, trading in carbon emissions reductions was legalized. A World Bank program, the first of its kind in the region, supports the implementation of state policies to reduce emissions in the energy sector.[28] The program will allow Uzbekistan to accumulate carbon credits and sell them on international carbon markets. For this purpose, a legal framework for carbon units and the national registry mechanism has been launched, which is a prerequisite to enter international carbon trading. In 2024–2025, the country launched pilot projects to account for and reduce emissions in the transport sector, including the introduction of carbon credits for projects related to the electrification of transport and the development of infrastructure for low-carbon fuels. The official launch of trading and the registry is scheduled for 1 January 2026. Small-scale carbon offset programs have been initiated in cooperation with Uzbekistan Railways and ADB particularly in logistics, including testing carbon credits for international freight corridors. These credits are targeted for sale in regional markets, such as the PRC's voluntary carbon market.

2.11. Conclusions on Carbon Pricing in CAREC Countries

Table 1 gives an overview of the status of carbon pricing in CAREC countries.

Table 1: Overview of Carbon Finance in CAREC Countries

Country	Carbon Tax	ETS	Carbon Market
Azerbaijan	No carbon tax; fuel subsidy level of around 40%	None	No domestic carbon market; registered projects in international markets but no transport projects
PRC	No carbon tax; general taxation level of 30%–40% on fuels	National and subnational ETS; transport sector partially included in some subnational ETS	National and subnational carbon markets with transport projects; international carbon credit projects with transport projects
Georgia	No carbon tax; general taxation level of 30%–40% on fuels	None	No domestic carbon market; registered projects in international markets but no transport projects
Kazakhstan	No carbon tax; fuel subsidy of 20%–45%[a]	National ETS without transport sector	Domestic carbon market linked with ETS; no projects in international markets
Kyrgyz Republic	No carbon tax; gasoline subsidy of around 10%	None	No domestic carbon market; no projects in international markets
Mongolia	No carbon tax; gasoline subsidy 10% and diesel tax of around 30%	None	No domestic carbon market; registered projects in international markets but no transport projects

continued on next page

[28] World Bank. 2024. Uzbekistan - Innovative Carbon Resource Application for Energy Transition (iCRAFT) Project.

Table 1 *continued*

Country	Carbon Tax	ETS	Carbon Market
Pakistan	No carbon tax; no subsidy or taxation	None	No domestic carbon market;[b] registered projects in international markets with one (and another in validation)[c]
Tajikistan	No carbon tax; tax of 10%–20% on fuels	None	No domestic carbon market; no projects in international markets
Turkmenistan	No carbon tax; fuel subsidy of 40%–50%	None	No domestic carbon market; no projects in international markets
Uzbekistan	No carbon tax; gasoline 10% subsidy and diesel 10% tax	None	No domestic carbon market; registered projects in international markets but no transport projects

CAREC = Central Asia Regional Economic Cooperation, PRC = People's Republic of China, ETS = emissions trading system.

Notes:

1. Status is as of end-2025; fuel subsidy/tax level is as of 2024 and excludes external economic effects.
2. Fuel subsidy levels are based on relation of explicit subsidy relative to supply cost and general taxation level is based on consumer price relative to supply cost.

[a] Lower level for diesel, higher level for gasoline.

[b] A domestic carbon market structure is proposed but not yet implemented as of October 2025.

[c] VERRA. Verified Carbon Standard (accessed 27 April 2026).

Source: International Monetary Fund. 2025. Data based on IMF Energy Subsidy Template Version December 2025; and authors' research of national documents.

Chapter 3

GHG EMISSION REDUCTION OPTIONS IN THE TRANSPORT SECTOR

This chapter discusses options for reducing GHG emissions in the transport sector in general and transport mitigation activities planned in CAREC countries.

3.1. GHG Mitigation Options

The framework of "Avoid–Shift–Improve–Fuels" provides a wide range of options available to reduce GHG emissions from the transport sector.[29] "Avoid" refers to reducing the number of trips or reducing trip distances, "shift" refers to changing from a high GHG-emitting transport mode to a low-emitting one, "improve" refers to reducing GHG emissions per unit of output, and "fuels" refers to changing from high GHG-emitting fuels to low GHG-emitting ones.

3.1.1. Policies

Multiple policy measures can affect GHG emissions of the transport sector.

Greenhouse Gas and Fuel Consumption Standards for Vehicles

Many countries have developed fuel consumption standards for vehicles. The targeted vehicle type is in general passenger cars, but standards have also been realized for light commercial and heavy-duty vehicles. Such standards result in reducing emissions per unit of distance and work like an ETS: The quantity is defined, and the targets are met, while the price for the target achievement is defined by the market. An important observation is that standards define emissions per unit of distance. International Council on Clean Transportation research indicates that fuel and GHG standards can generate more than half the emission reductions needed by the transport sector by 2050, i.e., this is a very important and impactful policy.[30] Absolute GHG emissions of vehicles can still increase due to higher vehicle sales and real-world GHG emissions being higher than those recorded under test conditions or with increased mileage. Increased mileage can be a consequence of improved fuel efficiency, as car users reduce fuel costs, making longer trips less expensive.

[29] This framework was developed by L. Shipper and his colleagues. World Bank. 1999. L. Schipper and C. Marie-Liliu. Transportation and CO_2 Emissions: Flexing the Link—A Path for the World Bank. *Climate Change Series.* No. 69.

[30] International Council on Clean Transportation (ICCT). Fuel Efficiency/CO_2 Emissions.

Zero-Emission Vehicle Mandates

Some countries have introduced zero-emission vehicle (ZEV) mandates, while others have them as targets.[31] The principle is that car manufacturers must sell a certain percentage of ZEVs each year with sales converted into tradable certificates, i.e., car manufacturers that do not reach targets can purchase certificates from those that do, or pay the penalty.[32] Certificates can be earned in the United Kingdom (UK) also with low-emission vehicles until 2029, e.g., with plug-in hybrids.[33] This effectively means that the ZEV targets are not necessarily met and makes the overall regulation function more like a technology-neutral CO_2 standard. The California ZEV mandate includes plug-in hybrid vehicles as ZEVs, which is problematic considering the questionable GHG impact of plug-in hybrid vehicles related to their limited battery size and limited electric charging, resulting in the overwhelming share of mileage being powered by fossil fuels.[34] Manufacturers generate tradable credits by selling ZEVs.

Many countries have also established targets for the phase out of internal combustion engines (ICEs).[35] These targets are set per vehicle category (e.g., Norway's phase out for 2025 is limited to light-duty vehicles),[36] are for vehicle sale rather than vehicle stock, and are subject to change. Also, the target is sometimes set as ICE phase out, and then as ZEV mandate, with ZEV having different definitions, including eventually the use of ICEs with e-fuels. In general, targets are also not mandatory, e.g., fossil cars can still be sold legally in Norway after 2025. ZEV targets or ICE phase-outs give important signals to vehicle manufacturers as well as purchasers, which can accelerate and drive EV adoption.

Fiscal and Normative Policies

Fiscal and normative policies influence either the usage level of vehicles or the vehicle purchase decision. Short-term reactions to price increases result in a reduced demand for the good (e.g., number or distance of trips or mode chosen) with the magnitude depending on the price elasticity of the good (e.g., business trips are less elastic than leisure trips).[37] Medium- to long-term reactions are to purchase a vehicle with lower total costs, e.g., fuel-efficient vehicles. Also, here the magnitude of impacts depends on price and income elasticities.

31 EVA England. ZEV Mandate; and Government of the United Kingdom. 2024. Pathway for Zero Emission Vehicle Transition by 2035 Becomes Law. 3 January.

32 The United Kingdom defines ZEVs as battery electric vehicles or fuel-cell electric vehicles (excluding plug-in hybrids and e-fuel powered vehicles).

33 ICCT. 2025. Flexibility or Uncertainty? Risks of the Proposed Changes to the UK Zero Emission Vehicle Mandate. 21 May.

34 California Air Resources Board. Zero-Emission Vehicle Regulation; See Transport & Environment. 2025. *Smoke Screen: The Growing PHEV Emissions Scandal*; A. Isenstadt et al. 2022. *Real World Usage of Plug-In Hybrid Vehicles in the United States*. ICCT; and P. Plötz et al. 2022. *Real-World Usage of Plug-In Hybrid Vehicles in Europe: A 2022 Update on Fuel Consumption, Electric Driving, and CO_2 Emissions*. ICCT.

35 S. H. Man. 2024. Electric Car Targets Compared Globally. *Compare the Market*. 16 December; and ZEV Transition Council. 2025. Phase-Out Targets: Cars and Vans. 22 December.

36 Hjem. Norwegian EV Policy.

37 C. Morlotti et al. 2017. Multi-Dimensional Price Elasticity for Leisure and Business Destinations in the Low-Cost Air Transport Market: Evidence from easyJet. *Tourism Management*. 61. pp. 23–34.

Policies that have an impact relate to fuel, car taxes, and registration policies. Fuel pricing policies can be uniform or discriminate between fuels, e.g., Switzerland has a lower tax on gaseous transport fuels than on liquid ones, and various countries impose differential fuel taxes for biofuels compared to fossil fuels. Over time, a higher fuel price will result in reduced fuel consumption, achieved through driving less and purchasing more efficient vehicles.[38] Car tax and registration policies are used in some countries, e.g., Singapore, to limit the number of private vehicles. The car tax can also be differentiated relative to GHG emissions, as is done in various European countries. The impact of a higher or differentiated car tax is to reduce the number of vehicles and to shift the fleet composition toward low GHG-emitting vehicles.

Vehicle Operating Regulations

Regulations can cover operating standards of vehicles, such as for inspections and maintenance, or for specific vehicle components, e.g., the EU introduced a mandatory labeling and phase-out regulation for tires, requiring more efficient ones—low rolling resistance tires reduce fuel consumption and therefore GHG emissions.

Road Pricing and Road Tax Policies

Distance- and weight-related road freight taxes are levied, e.g., in Germany or Switzerland, to promote a mode shift toward rail, to increase logistics efficiency (due to higher freight cost, empty backhaul is reduced) and to reduce distance and number of trips. Toll roads are also a form of road pricing, however they may not necessarily result in emissions reductions as drivers might opt to use roads without tolls, which can involve a detour or less fluid traffic conditions.

Zero-Emission and Congestion Zones, Vehicle Usage Regulations

Road or sector charging can be realized in urban areas to reduce congestion, as in London, Singapore, and Stockholm. Regulations can also specify zones based on emission standards (low or zero-emission zones), thus creating incentives for low-emitting vehicles. This can be based on pollution standards (e.g., Mexico) with no or marginal GHG impact, or on various pollutants. The entry of specific vehicle types can also be managed, e.g., the ban of motorcycles in many cities of the PRC and the prohibition of gasoline motorcycles in downtown Ha Noi planned for mid-2026. Vehicle usage regulations can include special lanes for multiple occupancy vehicles (combined in many countries with ZEVs) or special lanes for public transport vehicles (Section 3.1.2). Other measures to reduce GHG emissions in urban areas, such as parking management, can promote the usage of low GHG vehicles, encourage mode shift, and reduce private motorized traffic.

[38] For a discussion of fuel price elasticities see Section 4.1.

Policy-Based Crediting in Carbon Markets

As of the end of 2025, carbon market projects traded in compliance or voluntary markets through carbon market standards are based on project- or program-based approaches, where a direct cause-and-effect relation between specific investment actions and the resultant GHG reduction can be shown. The impact of policies however will depend on many other influencing factors.[39] Policy crediting issues carbon credits from the implementation of one or more policy instruments, rather than from individual projects or programs. Article 6 of the Paris Agreement permits policy crediting while the market mechanisms of the Kyoto Protocol did not cater to this option. Complexities of such approaches are related to methodological challenges in terms of determining additionality and establishing a crediting baseline, attribution, and credit ownership issues. Results of policies should be directly attributable to the policy instrument implemented. The Gold Standard under its pilot policy program has listed indicative policies and their applicability to this scheme: ETS, carbon taxes, fossil fuel taxes, vehicle emission standards, fuel blending mandates, and technology and/or performance and energy efficiency standards are all expected to be non-eligible.[40] Indicative eligible policies are risk-sharing instruments, removal of policies posing a technology restriction, and removal of planned financial subsidies or subsidies and/or incentives. The Gold Standard requires policy programs to perform a financial additionality test comparable to project-based approaches.[41] The impact and carbon credits are given at activity-level and are not based on a macroeconomic assessment. Policy-based activities as defined by the Gold Standard could also have been developed under a Program of Activities or as individual projects with the existing framework.

A different approach is taken by the Transformative Carbon Asset Facility, a trust fund administered by the World Bank (Box 1).[42]

39 For a discussion of different approaches see World Bank. 2025. *Carbon Crediting: A Results-Based Approach to Mobilizing Additional Climate Financing*.

40 Gold Standard for the Global Goals. 2024. *Policy Requirements and Procedures*.

41 See Gold Standard for the Global Goals. 2024. *Determining Additionality of a Policy*.

42 See Transformative Carbon Asset Facility. Who We Are.

Box 1: Uzbekistan iCRAFT Project

The Innovative Carbon Resource Application for Energy Transition Project for Uzbekistan (iCRAFT) is the World Bank's first "policy crediting" program. iCRAFT aims to create incentives to gradually reduce energy subsidies to lower energy consumption and greenhouse gas emissions. iCRAFT received a $46 million grant from the Transformative Carbon Asset Facility (TCAF) which was used to help mitigate the impact of the increase in energy prices foreseen until 2026. A first results-based payment based on verified emissions reductions was made in June 2024 with a price of $15 per verified emissions reduction. In the second phase, internationally transferred mitigation outcomes (ITMOs) will also be generated by the project with a price of $30/t$CO_2$.[a]

The assessment of additionality as well as the baseline setting of the TCAF are not in line with the Gold Standard approach and are not an internationally recognized approach.[b] The project design document has no elaborate additionality determination.[c] The methodology was developed by TCAF specifically for the program with validation and verification made by the same entity (Aenor) which is also not in line with international carbon market standards (footnote c).

As such, this is an interesting approach and program and possible under Article 6.2 of the Paris Agreement as ITMOs transferred under this article do not require an internationally approved methodology; countries negotiate directly with one another the terms of their cooperative approaches. A policy-based program is however deemed to be relatively complex to operationalize under Article 6.4 or for international carbon markets operating under existing standards.

a For program details see World Bank. 2023. International Bank for Reconstruction and Development Project Appraisal Document on a Proposed Grant in the Amount of US$46.25 million to the Republic of Uzbekistan for the Innvoative Carbon Resource Application for Energy Transition Project. Cited prices for verified emissions reductions are in para. 37 and for ITMOs in para. 44.

b See for a critical review A. Michaelowa and J. Kessler. 2024. Methodological Challenges of Policy Crediting Under Article 6 of the Paris Agreement. Perspectives Climate Research gGmbH.

c AENOR. 2024. *TCAF Verification Report*.

Source: Compiled by author.

3.1.2. Urban Transport

Cities are a major contributor to climate change with estimates suggesting that they are responsible for 70% of global carbon emissions, with transport and buildings among the largest contributors.[43] Over 1,000 cities have committed to net-zero targets.[44] Reduction of urban transport GHG emissions is thus a major issue. While urban transport challenges focus often on issues such as air quality, congestion, and mobility, GHG emissions are also becoming a core element.

Public Transport Supply

Multiple projects have been realized in this area, including large-scale investments in new mass rapid transit systems such as bus rapid transit, metros, light-rail transit (LRT), trams, and urban cable cars. Public transport projects can also include the improvement and upgrading of existing systems, e.g., through integrated and smart ticketing, improved vehicle dispatch, and mode integration.

43 United Nations Environment Programme (UNEP). Cities and Climate Change.

44 C40 Cities. Cities Race to Zero.

Urban Freight

Most freight emissions are generally caused by inter-urban traffic. However, efforts are also necessary to curb urban freight transport emissions through logistics measures such as freight consolidation centers. Some cities also envisage low-carbon or electric urban freight vehicles.

Nonmotorized Transport

Nonmotorized transport (NMT) programs have been linked in many countries with climate finance. NMT projects include infrastructure such as bike lanes or bike-sharing programs.

Zero-Emission Zones and Congestion Zone Charging

Zero- or low-emission zones have been created in various cities, with a focus on local pollutants. However, recently GHG criteria have also entered the picture, with cities demanding, for example, EVs or similar vehicles that can operate in electric mode for a specific driving range. GHG emissions reductions are due to low-emitting GHG vehicles as well as avoided trips. See Section 2.1.1 on policies.

Congestion zone charging has been established in London and Singapore, for example, targeting reduced congestion. They result in reduced GHG emissions through mode shift and improved traffic flow albeit this better flow can then lead again to increasing traffic volumes.

For both instruments, GHG emissions reduction is in general not the primary target; rather, the target is a reduction of pollutants and congestion.

Intelligent Transport Systems and Information and Communication Technology

Intelligent transport systems can provide information to commuters, visitors, and businesses before and after trips. GHG emissions reductions can be achieved through less congestion (resulting in higher average speeds and therefore less fuel consumption) and reduced distances driven. Information and communication technology can also be used within various modes of urban public transport to improve system efficiency and management.

General Alignment of Carbon Pricing with Urban Mitigation Activities

Carbon pricing and urban projects are primarily linked through carbon markets, which can only be used effectively in well-defined individual projects, such as public transport supply projects, where methodologies exist to determine the attributable GHG impact.[45] In some cases, e.g., NMT projects, the directly measurable and attributable emissions reductions are generally too small to warrant the costs involved in structuring and monitoring a carbon credit project.

[45] Carbon taxes as well as ETS are established in general at the national or regional level, not at the urban level.

3.1.3. Rail and Shipping

Rail, shipping, and pipelines transporting liquid fuels are, in general, low-carbon modes of transport for passengers and freight.[46] Emissions reductions result due to mode shift, e.g., road to rail or aviation to rail. There are also projects to improve the efficiency and reduce emissions of rail and shipping, e.g., electrification of services.

Rail and Shipping Supply

Rail investment projects include the implementation of high-speed rail, new lines, double-tracking of tracks, infrastructure improvements such as signalling, which can increase track capacity, resulting in more attractive passenger and freight services.[47] Shipping projects include investments in ports and in improving the navigability of rivers to increase domestic shipping.

Efficiency Improvements

Various rail and shipping operational efficiency improvements to reduce GHG emissions can be implemented. Projects in rail efficiency include retrofitting common rail direct injection systems on diesel locomotives and retrofitting locomotors with auxiliary power units, which allows the main engine to shut down, thus reducing idling time and wasted fuel. Swiss Federal Railways (SBB) has realized eco drive (an efficient driving procedure) on selected rail routes to reduce its carbon footprint. In shipping, multiple energy efficiency measures include design measures (e.g., air lubrication), propulsion measures (e.g., propeller modifications), machinery measures (e.g., engine tuning), and advanced hull surface coatings. Logistics improvements can result in more attractive services and thus a modal shift toward rail or shipping.

Low-Carbon Fuels and Electrification

Alternate fuels for ships and trains include biofuels, biogas, electrification, and e-fuels based on green hydrogen. For example, electric ferries are becoming increasingly competitive for short and medium distances, with multiple projects being implemented in this area.

General Alignment of Carbon Pricing with Rail and Shipping Projects

Carbon pricing can foster rail and shipping projects through carbon taxes on transport fuels, which make low-carbon transport modes such as rail and shipping more competitive and encourage their electrification. Also, carbon markets can cater to rail and shipping projects, although at the moment this sector lacks approved methodologies in many areas.

46 See for example European Environment Agency. 2021. *Rail and Waterborne—Best for Low-Carbon Motorised Transport*; International Energy Agency. Rail; and S. Forman. *Emissions from Rail vs Trucking*. Coursework submitted for Physics of Energy.

47 For an example of new dedicated rail freight corridors in India, see Government of India, Ministry of Railways. 2025. Ministry of Railways Advances Infrastructure with Dedicated Freight Corridors, Modernization Initiatives, and Enhanced Freight Capacity. News release. 19 March.

3.1.4. Low-Carbon Vehicles and Fuels

While an increasing number of countries have formulated overall net-zero GHG emissions reduction targets, net-zero or zero GHG road maps specifically for the transport sector are less common. Reviewing such road maps, a common feature can be observed: while efficiency measures, mode shift, traffic avoidance, etc. are listed as measures, all countries rely on ZEVs dominated by EVs for road transport and alternate fuels for shipping and aviation to achieve zero emissions.[48]

General Alignment of Carbon Pricing with Low-Carbon Vehicles and Fuels

Carbon pricing plays a central role in fostering low-carbon vehicles and fuels, either through carbon taxes, which can foster for instance biofuels (Section 4.1), ETS, e.g., tradable ZEV credits (Section 4.2.), or carbon market projects (EV projects as of the end of 2025 are the most popular transport project type in carbon markets) (Section 4.3).

3.2. Overview of Transport Measures in CAREC Countries

This section focuses on transport mitigation options under discussion and development in CAREC countries as well as NDC discussions. The information is based on interviews with representatives from governments, NDC documents, and national transport publications.

Azerbaijan

In 2022, Azerbaijan had total GHG emissions excluding land-use change and forestry (LUCF) of around 58.8 million tons of CO_2 ($MtCO_2$), of which the transport sector accounted for 9.4 $MtCO_2$ or 16%. Over the 2 decades until the end of 2022, transportation emissions had an average annual compound growth rate of 7%, while total GHG emissions in the same period "only" increased by 2.2%.[49] Azerbaijan's NDC 3.0 focuses on electrification generated by renewable energy sources, biofuels, and energy efficiency.[50] Specific mitigation measures included in Azerbaijan's NDC are reducing congestion through building road infrastructure, expanding railway transport for passenger and freight transport, developing and expanding a metro network, encouraging eco-driving, renewing the national aviation fleet, updating vehicle emission standards (to meet EU standards), and boosting the electrification of transport and usage of biofuels.

People's Republic of China

In 2022, the PRC had total GHG emissions excluding LUCF of around 13.36 $GtCO_2$, of which the transport sector accounted for 0.91 $GtCO_2$ or 7%. Transportation emissions had an average annual compound growth rate for the 2 decades until the end of 2022 of 6% while total GHG emissions in

48 See for example Changing Transport. NDC Transport Tracker.

49 Based on Climate Watch. Historical GHG Emissions (accessed 15 October 2025).

50 Government of the Republic of Azerbaijan. 2025. *Azerbaijan's Nationally Determined Contributions 3.0*.

the same period increased by 4.9%. The PRC's updated NDC 3.0 includes pledges to boost the use of low-carbon transport, including through improving green transportation systems and standards, fostering low-carbon urban mobility, e.g., through stronger public transport and NMT, increasing rail and water transportation for passengers and freight, promoting low-carbon fuels, and encouraging EVs.[51] NDC 3.0 puts particular emphasis on EVs, public transport, electric shore power for ships (cold ironing), electrification of railways, and sustainable aviation fuel.[52]

Georgia

In 2022, Georgia had total GHG emissions excluding LUCF of around 19.2 $MtCO_2$, of which the transport sector accounted for 4.5 $MtCO_2$ or 23%. Transportation emissions had an average annual compound growth rate for the 2 decades until the end of 2022 of 6.6% while total GHG emissions in the same period increased by 2.7% (footnote 49). In its NDC 3.0, Georgia targets reduce GHG emissions 47% below 1990 levels by 2030, with an extended target of 50% by 2035. It plans to cut GHG emissions from the transport sector by 20% from the reference level by 2030.[53] The NDC includes transport mitigation measures in the areas of urban transport, rail, alternative fuels, and low-or zero-emission vehicles. The government plans to introduce changes to the tax code to increase registration rates for vehicles older than 6 years with the target of accelerating fleet renewal.[54]

Kazakhstan

In 2022, Kazakhstan had total GHG emissions excluding LUCF of around 331 $MtCO_2$, of which the transport sector accounted for 25 $MtCO_2$ or 8%. Transportation emissions had an average annual compound growth rate for the 2 decades until the end of 2022 of 4.9% while total GHG emissions in the same period increased by 2.3% (footnote 49). The Development Strategy of the Republic of Kazakhstan until 2050, along with the National Development Plan until 2025 and the Action Plan for the implementation of the Concept for the Transition to a "Green Economy" for 2021–2030, all support Kazakhstan's NDC goals,[55] which include measures for sustainable transport and the development of infrastructure for electric and gas vehicles.[56] The NDC 3.0 includes transport as a key area of mitigation, focusing on modernization and electrification of transport and low-carbon mobility (footnote 55). Projected GHG transport emissions under a business-as-usual (BAU) scenario are expected to increase from 30 to 35 $MtCO_2$ from 2025 to 2035. The NDC 3.0 targets an unconditional GHG reduction of 15% by 2030 and of 17% by 2035 relative to 1990. Kazakhstan has integrated sustainable transport development goals into its national strategies, including low-carbon development, aiming to increase the share of electric and hybrid vehicles to 30% by 2030. The country targets achieving carbon neutrality by 2060.

51 Government of the People's Republic of China, Ministry of Ecology and Environment. 2021. *PRC's Achievements, New Goals, and New Measures for Nationally Determined Contributions*.

52 Government of the People's Republic of China. 2025. *PRC's NDC Report 2035*. In Mandarin.

53 Government of Georgia, Ministry of Environmental Protection and Agriculture. 2026. *Georgia's Nationally Determined Contribution (NDC) 3.0*.

54 *Interpress News*. 2026. The Ruling Team's Initiative to Increase Customs Duties on Cars Older than 6 Years has been Introduced in Parliament. 16 March.

55 Government of the Republic of Kazakhstan, Ministry of Ecology and Natural Resources. 2025. *Nationally Determined Contribution of the Republic of Kazakhstan to the Global Response to Climate Change Until 2035*.

56 International Energy Agency. 2022. *Concept for the Transition of the Republic of Kazakhstan to a "Green Economy."*

Kyrgyz Republic

In 2022, the Kyrgyz Republic had total GHG emissions excluding LUCF of around 17.5 $MtCO_2$, of which the transport sector accounted for 1.5 $MtCO_2$ or 9%. Transportation emissions had an average annual compound growth rate for the 2 decades until the end of 2022 of 3.1% while total GHG emissions in the same period increased by 2.9% (footnote 49). For transport, the NDC 3.0 prioritizes increasing the share of low-emission vehicles, developing alternative transport, developing bicycle infrastructure, and implementing automated traffic management systems.[57] Unconditional measures included are increasing the number of compressed natural gas-powered vehicles and conducting a feasibility study on a fuel tax. If the study shows positive results, the plan is to introduce a 10% fuel tax on gasoline and a 4% tax on diesel. Conditional measures include increasing the number of EVs, increasing the number of electric scooters and bicycles, developing cycle lanes, and introducing automated traffic management systems at intersections.

Mongolia

In 2022, Mongolia had total GHG emissions excluding LUCF of around 59 $MtCO_2$, of which the transport sector accounted for 3.2 $MtCO_2$ or 5%. Transportation emissions had an average annual compound growth rate for the 2 decades until the end of 2022 of 5.5% while total GHG emissions in the same period increased by 4.2% (footnote 49). Mongolia's NDC 3.0 does not include specific mitigation measures for the transport sector.[58] Mongolia's first updated NDC (2022) targets reducing GHG emissions for transport relative to BAU emissions by 1.05 $MtCO_2$ by 2030, equivalent to 6% of the total target figure. The transport reduction shall be achieved through (i) switching to Euro 5 fuels, (ii) mode switching road to rail for coal exports, and (iii) switching passenger heating of railways to electric heating.

Pakistan

In 2024, Pakistan had total GHG emissions of around 585 $MtCO_2$.[59] The transport sector accounts for around 12% of emissions. Transportation emissions had an average annual compound growth rate for the 2 decades until the end of 2022 of 4.1% while total GHG emissions in the same period increased by 3.4%. Pakistan's NDC 3.0 calls for accelerated deployment of EVs and upgrading of vehicle emission standards (to Euro standards). Thirty percent of new vehicle sales are targeted to be electric by 2030 and 3,000 charging stations should be added by 2030. For shipping and aviation, the usage of low-carbon fuels is planned. Pakistan also plans to upgrade its railway network and its public transport, particularly in urban areas. Urban transport projects with e-buses and also rail expansion are being supported by ADB.

[57] Government of the Kyrgyz Republic. 2025. Nationally Determined Contribution of the Kyrgyz Republic (NDC). In Russian.
[58] Government of Mongolia. 2025. *Nationally Determined Contribution (NDC 3.0) of Mongolia*.
[59] Government of Pakistan. 2025. *Pakistan's Third Nationally Determined Contribution (NDC 3.0)*.

Tajikistan

In 2022, Tajikistan had total GHG emissions excluding LUCF of around 18.7 $MtCO_2$, of which the transport sector accounted for 2.3 $MtCO_2$ or 12%. Transportation emissions had an average annual compound growth rate for the 2 decades until the end of 2022 of 15% while total GHG emissions in the same period increased by 5%. The NDC emphasizes a shift toward electric mobility and sustainable transport infrastructure.[60] NDC 3.0 is planned to be submitted by December 2026. Tajikistan's Green Economy Development Strategy (2023–2037) aims to have 55% of all vehicles in Tajikistan electric by 2037.

Turkmenistan

In 2022, Turkmenistan had total GHG emissions excluding LUCF of around 215 $MtCO_2$, of which the transport sector accounted for 11.3 $MtCO_2$ or 5%. Transportation emissions had an average annual compound growth rate for the 2 decades until the end of 2022 of 2% while total GHG emissions in the same period increased by 3%. The NDC includes as key measures impacting the transport sector the development of public transport, fleet renewal, clean fuels, and efficiency improvements and electrification in railway transport.[61] With support of United Nations agencies, the country is finalizing its NDC 3.0.

Uzbekistan

In 2022, Uzbekistan had total GHG emissions excluding LUCF of around 190 $MtCO_2$, of which the transport sector accounted for 18.6 $MtCO_2$ or 10%. Transportation emissions had an average annual compound growth rate for the 2 decades until the end of 2022 of 1.5% while total GHG emissions in the same period increased by 0.2%. Uzbekistan promotes electric transport and targets converting 80% of public transport vehicles to gas and electricity by 2030. Its NDC 3.0 plans to reduce GHG transport emissions by 2.5 $MtCO_2$ relative to the baseline by 2035 through electrification of railways, development and electrification of public transport, and environmentally friendly vehicles.[62]

Summary

Table 2 summarizes the main transport mitigation measures planned or undertaken in CAREC countries.

[60] Government of the Republic of Tajikistan. 2021. *Updated NDC of the Republic of Tajikistan*.
[61] Government of Turkmenistan. 2022. *Nationally Determined Contribution of Turkmenistan under the Paris Agreement*.
[62] Centre of Hydrometeorological Service. 2016. *Third National Communication of the Republic of Uzbekistan under the UNFCCC*.

Table 2: Overview of Planned Transport Mitigation Measures for CAREC Countries, as of end-2025

Country	EVs	Rail Expansion/ Electrification	Public Transport and NMT	Compressed Natural Gas and Biofuels	Other
Azerbaijan	✓	✓	✓	✓	Road expansion
PRC	✓	✓	✓		SAF
Georgia	✓		✓		
Kazakhstan	✓			✓	
Kyrgyz Republic	✓	✓	✓		Automated traffic management systems
Mongolia		✓	✓	✓	Vehicle emission standards
Pakistan	✓	✓	✓		Vehicle emission standards
Tajikistan	✓				
Turkmenistan	✓	✓	✓		
Uzbekistan	✓	✓	✓	✓	

Green cell: Measure is included.
CAREC = Central Asia Regional Economic Cooperation, PRC = People's Republic of China, EV = electric vehicle, NMT = nonmotorized transport, SAF = sustainable aviation fuel.
Source: Authors' examination of nationally determined contribution documents from member governments.

Chapter 4

CARBON TAXES

This chapter examines carbon taxes as an instrument then explores their application to the transport sector in general and CAREC countries in particular.

4.1. Carbon Tax Instrument

A carbon tax sets a price on GHG emissions. In general, it is levied on the carbon content of fossil fuel, but it can also be levied on other GHGs, e.g., methane emissions. Carbon taxes are commonly applied across an entire economy, upon specific sectors, or on specific products, e.g., on fuels used in the transport sector. Carbon taxes can be implemented at a national or subnational level, e.g., Canada or Mexico have different levels of carbon taxes at provincial or state levels. Some subnational jurisdictions have implemented and then abolished carbon taxes, especially in North America.

As of April 2025, the 43 economies or subnational jurisdictions had implemented carbon taxes, with the first to do so being Poland and Finland in 1990. In Asia, only Japan; Singapore (Box 2); and Taipei,China have implemented a carbon tax. Indonesia, Malaysia, Thailand, and Viet Nam are considering or preparing a carbon tax. As of the end of 2025, no CAREC country has a carbon tax.

Carbon tax levels vary considerably, ranging from $0.10 per tCO_2 in Poland to $159 per tCO_2 in Uruguay (Figure 2). Western European countries and Uruguay have the highest levels of taxes. In general, carbon taxes only cover a share of the GHG emissions of the jurisdiction in which they are enforced. For example, Uruguay's carbon tax, implemented in January 2022 through presidential decree, is only charged on gasoline fuel, at around $0.30 per liter (L).[63] The tax replaced partially an existing excise tax without increasing the tax burden, i.e., the structure of the excise tax applied to gasoline was modified to include a component linked to carbon emissions of the fuel. As of the end of 2025, the gasoline price in Uruguay is 60% higher than for diesel, which has lower excise taxes and no carbon tax.[64] Another example is the Swiss carbon tax, which covers 35% of emissions, is limited to CO_2, and is not applied to transport fuels. Nevertheless, the gasoline price in Switzerland is higher than in Uruguay due to excise taxes. Most countries today levy taxes on transport fuel, which have

[63] Government of Uruguay. 2022. *Fijacion Del Imesi a la Primera Enajenacion de Combustibles*. In Spanish.

[64] Such differential fuel taxes have been a major reason for the dieselization of vehicle fleets in Europe, which has resulted in massive particle matter and nitrogen oxide air quality problems.

Box 2: Singapore Carbon Tax

The carbon tax in Singapore was levied in January 2019 and covers all six greenhouse gases (GHGs), with a coverage of around 70% of GHG emissions. The carbon tax is levied on facilities with more than 50,000 tons of carbon dioxide (tCO_2) emissions in the manufacturing, power, waste, and water sectors. It is not levied on transport fuels, though Singapore has a relatively high excise tax, especially on gasoline. An interesting feature of the Singaporean carbon tax is its staged pricing. The price started at S$5 per tCO_2, moving to S$25 in 2024, reached S$45 in 2026, and aims to reach S$50–S$80 by 2028.

Another interesting feature is that companies may use international carbon credits under Article 6 of the Paris Agreement to offset up to 5% of their taxable emissions. From 2024 onward, Singapore to this purpose has established bilateral agreements with many countries and has recently launched a second call for project proposals from one of the 10 countries where implementation agreements have already been signed.

Sources: National Climate Change Secretariat Singapore. Carbon Tax; Carbon Trading. Singapore's Article 6 Cooperation; and Government of Singapore, Ministry of Trade and Industry. 2025. Singapore Launches Second Request for Proposals for High Quality Carbon Credits. News release. 31 October.

impact to carbon taxes an impact on fuel usage.[65] Traditional fuel taxes are however not related to the carbon content of fuels—it is typical for example to levy a lower tax on diesel than gasoline, even though the carbon content of diesel is higher than of gasoline. Fuel taxes, including excise taxes as well as general sales taxes and other fees imposed on fuels, could be rebranded as carbon taxes—the impact on CO_2 emissions will be the same, no matter the name of the tax.

Annual government revenues from carbon taxes range from $2 million (Estonia 2024) to $7.8 billion (France 2024), with eight countries having annual carbon tax revenues exceeding $1 billion. In some countries, carbon taxes, or more commonly a portion of carbon taxes, can be offset by regulated entities with carbon credits. Chilean regulated entities can offset completely their carbon taxes, while Colombia and Singapore have set maximum shares of emissions that can be offset.[66] Sweden does not allow any.

Multiple studies have been conducted on the impact of carbon taxes. A recent study commissioned by the European Central Bank covering more than 50 countries with carbon taxes found that territorial emissions (emissions emitted within a country's borders) were reduced with carbon taxes at a rate of roughly 0.1% reduction in emissions per implied dollar price per ton of carbon.[67] However, carbon taxes had no significant impact on consumption emissions, which can be considered as "carbon leakage"[68]

65 Based on a gasoline price without taxes using as reference the US gasoline price excluding taxes.

66 Ministerio del Medio Ambiente. Preguntas Frecuentes. In Spanish.

67 C. Schroeder and L. Stracca. 2023. Pollution Havens? Carbon Taxes, Globalization, and the Geography of Emissions. *ECB Working Paper Series*. No. 2862. European Central Bank.

68 Emissions may shift to locations in which they face no or lower taxes.

(emissions emitted anywhere in the world to satisfy domestic demand).[69] This suggests a limited global GHG impact of national carbon taxes in isolation. National carbon taxes can thus only have a meaningful impact if the production of emissions cannot be reallocated across borders without significant costs. A carbon tax on fuels used in housing or transportation, for example, cannot or can only partially be reallocated effectively across borders, whereas carbon taxes imposed on goods or other industries can be more easily reallocated. This needs to be considered when designing a carbon tax policy, as the tax can have negative economic and social domestic impacts due to potentially provoking a shift of carbon-intensive industries and jobs toward countries with lower or no carbon taxes.

Figure 2: Carbon Tax per Country, 1 April 2025

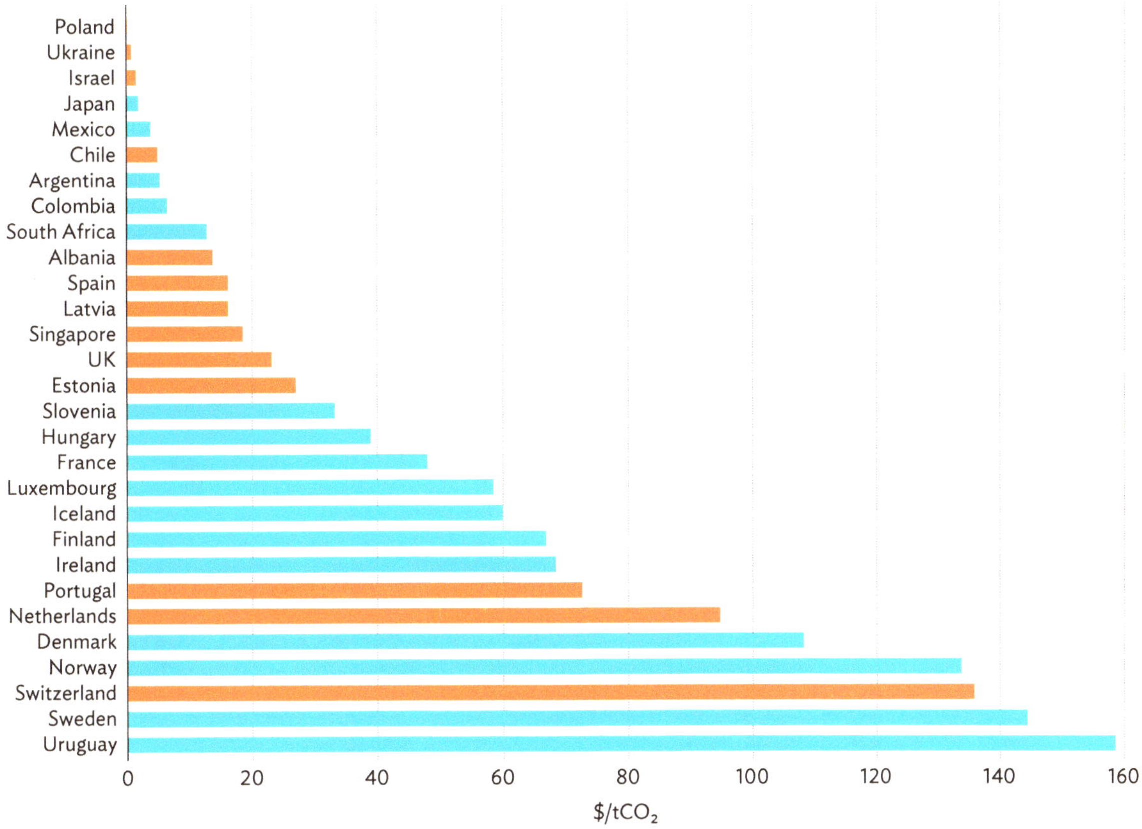

tCO_2 = tons of carbon dioxide, UK = United Kingdom.
Note: Orange refers to carbon tax not levied on transport fuels; blue refers to carbon tax levied on transport fuels plus (with exception of Uruguay) on other sectors.
Source: World Bank Group. State and Trends of Carbon Pricing Dashboard (accessed 27 April 2026).

[69] The concept of carbon leakage is well established. See e.g., B. R. Copeland, J. S. Shapiro, and M. S. Taylor. 2022. Globalization and the Environment. *Handbook of International Economics*. 5. pp. 61–146. For empirical evidence see R. Aichele and G. Felbermayr. 2015. Kyoto and Carbon Leakage: An Empirical Analysis of the Carbon Content of Bilateral Trade. *Review of Economics and Statistics*. 97 (1). pp. 104–15; J. Böning, V. di Nino, and T. Folger. 2023. The EU Must Stop Carbon Leakage at the Border to Become Climate Neutral. *VoxEU.org*. 8 August; M. L. Fowlie and M. Reguant. 2022. Mitigating Emissions Leakage in Incomplete Carbon Markets. *Journal of the Association of Environmental and Resource Economists*. 9 (2). pp. 307–343; and D. R. Känzig, J. Marenz, and M. Olbert. 2024. Carbon Leakage to Developing Countries.

Carbon tax revenues can be recycled back to GHG mitigation projects, thereby further increasing the impact of the carbon tax. This is done for example in Switzerland, where, as of the end of 2025, half of CO_2 tax revenues are used for investments in climate mitigation projects and the other half is paid out to residents on a per capita base via the compulsory national health insurance system.

4.2. Carbon Tax in Transportation—CAREC Countries

As of 2025, around 20 countries levy a carbon tax on transport fuels, with rates ranging from \$2/tCO_2 (Japan) to \$159/tCO_2 (Uruguay). This amounts to a tax of between \$0.01 and \$0.60/L for diesel and \$0.01 and \$0.66/L for gasoline. Transport fuels however are already taxed in most countries—in Uruguay, the carbon tax specifically partially substituted a former fuel tax. The impact of a "standard" fuel tax and a carbon fuel tax is essentially the same; a standard tax simply has an indirect GHG impact as its goal is not to reduce GHG emissions but rather, for instance, to finance road infrastructure. Therefore, Figures 3 and 4 show the explicit subsidy or tax on gasoline and diesel fuels in CAREC countries to indicate the existing level of taxation (which could be rebranded as a carbon tax).

Figure 3: Gasoline Explicit Subsidy or Tax in CAREC Countries, 2024

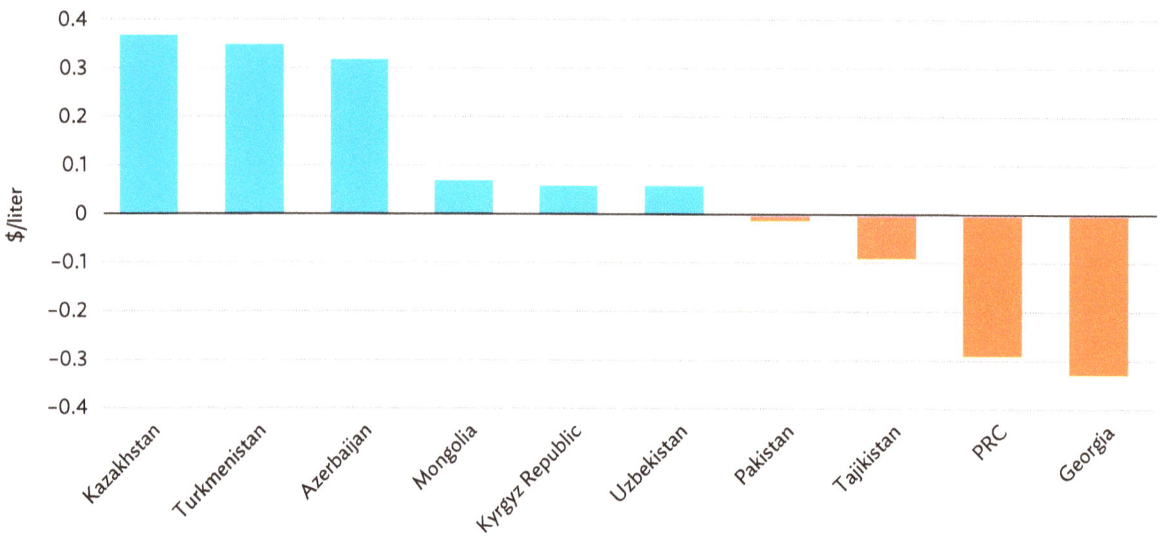

CAREC = Central Asia Regional Economic Cooperation, PRC = People's Republic of China.
Note: "Explicit subsidy" is the consumer price minus fuel cost; "tax" is the cost minus consumer price and does not include external costs of fuels.
Source: Data based on IMF Energy Subsidy Template Version 12/2025; for sources and definitions see S. Black et al. 2025. Underpriced and Overused: Fossil Fuel Subsidies Data 2025 Update. *IMF Working Papers*. No. 2025/270. International Monetary Fund.

In 2024, Azerbaijan, Kazakhstan, the Kyrgyz Republic, Mongolia, Turkmenistan, and Uzbekistan had explicit subsidies on gasoline, while other CAREC countries taxed fuels. All countries had implicit subsidies on fuels, considering the external costs of global warming, local air pollution, and vehicle externalities due to usage of fossil fuels. Table 3 shows how these fuel prices can be translated into a carbon tax. The PRC and Georgia had implicit carbon taxes on gasoline of more than $100/tCO$_2$.

Table 3: Implicit Carbon Tax on Gasoline Fuels in CAREC Countries, 2024

Country	Implicit Carbon Tax on Gasoline ($/ton of carbon dioxide)
Kazakhstan	(163)
Turkmenistan	(154)
Azerbaijan	(141)
Mongolia	(31)
Kyrgyz Republic	(26)
Uzbekistan	(26)
Pakistan	4
Tajikistan	40
People's Republic of China	128
Georgia	145

( ) = negative, CAREC = Central Asia Regional Economic Cooperation.
Note: Carbon tax is calculated based on 2.27 kilograms of carbon dioxide (CO_2) per liter of gasoline, based on the Intergovernmental Panel on Climate Change values for the net calorific value and the CO_2 emission factor of of gasoline.
Source: Authors' calculations based on IMF Energy Subsidy Template Version 12/2025 and S. Black et al. 2025. Underpriced and Overused: Fossil Fuel Subsidies Data 2025 Update. *IMF Working Papers*. No. 2025/270. International Monetary Fund.

Figure 4: Diesel Explicit Subsidy or Tax in CAREC Countries, 2024

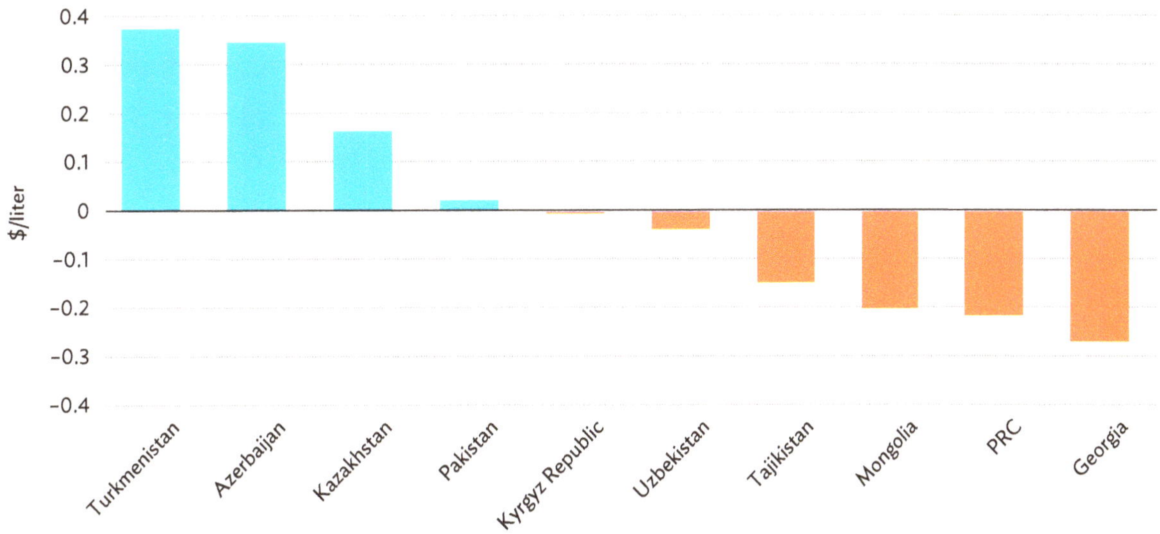

CAREC = Central Asia Regional Economic Cooperation, PRC = People's Republic of China.
Note: "Explicit subsidy" is the consumer price minus fuel cost; "tax" is the cost minus consumer price and does not include external costs of fuels.
Source: Data based on IMF Energy Subsidy Template Version 12/2025; for sources and definitions see S. Black et al. 2025. Underpriced and Overused: Fossil Fuel Subsidies Data 2025 Update. *IMF Working Papers*. No. 2025/270. International Monetary Fund.

As of the end of 2025, Azerbaijan, Kazakhstan, Pakistan, and Turkmenistan explicitly subsidize diesel. Table 4 shows how these fuel prices can be translated into a carbon tax.

Table 4: Implicit Carbon Tax on Diesel Fuels in CAREC Countries, mid-2024

Country	Implicit Carbon Tax on Diesel ($/ton of carbon dioxide)
Turkmenistan	(138)
Azerbaijan	(126)
Kazakhstan	(59)
Pakistan	(7)
Kyrgyz Republic	4
Uzbekistan	15
Tajikistan	56
Mongolia	74
People's Republic of China	78
Georgia	100

( ) = negative, CAREC = Central Asia Regional Economic Cooperation.
Note: Carbon tax calculations are based on 2.69 kilograms of carbon dioxide (CO_2) per liter of diesel, based on the Intergovernmental Panel on Climate Change values for the net calorific value and the CO_2 emission factor of diesel.
Source: Authors' calculations based on IMF Energy Subsidy Template Version 12/2025 and S. Black et al. 2025. Underpriced and Overused: Fossil Fuel Subsidies Data 2025 Update. *IMF Working Papers*. No. 2025/270. International Monetary Fund.

Not surprisingly, taxation levels are in general lower on diesel fuels than on gasoline fuels based on arguments that diesel is predominantly used by trucks and public transport. However, in 2024, the PRC, Georgia, Mongolia, and Tajikistan had implicit carbon taxes on diesel fuel of more than $50/t$CO_2$.

The direct GHG impact of transport fuel taxes is limited due to the inelastic demand for gasoline, estimated in the short term to be −0.02 to −0.04.[70] This means that to achieve a demand reduction (equivalent to CO_2 reduction) of 1%, a 25%–50% increase in the price of petrol would be required. With EVs increasingly being an alternative to fossil-fuel vehicles, in the medium- and long-term elasticity is expected to be larger. In the short term, the consumer can only reduce distances driven or change their mode of transit, with these limited choices resulting in low short-term elasticity. In the medium- and long-term, however, the consumer has more options and can, for example, opt for vehicles with better fuel economy or EVs.[71] This means that carbon taxes can be an instrument to spur adoption of EVs.

[70] US Energy Information Administration. 2014. Today in Energy: Gasoline Prices Tend to Have Little Effect on Demand for Car Travel. 17 December.

[71] Medium-term elasticity is related to the vehicle owner having the option to purchase low-fuel usage vehicles. EVs are one option. Higher fuel prices make EVs relatively more competitive, spur their sales, and thus reduce fossil fuel consumption, the price elasticity of fuel price increases. See Y. Fey et al. 2025. Does High Gasoline Price Spur Electric Vehicle Adoption? Evidence from Chinese Cities. *Energy Economics*. 142.

Another approach is used in Switzerland, where a levy of around \$0.015/L was imposed by the association of fuel importers on all gasoline and diesel sales between 2005 and 2012.[72] Since then, a similar system has been used but with a higher levy (as of the end of 2025 around \$0.05/L). Funds raised from the levy are used to finance CO_2 reduction projects domestically and abroad, i.e., the levy proceeds are used to purchase carbon credits. The impact is twofold: a slight reduction of fuel consumption and direct fuel-related GHG emissions (only slight as price elasticity is low), plus more importantly, a GHG emissions reduction due to investments realized in domestic and international carbon credits. For example, Switzerland used approximately 4.5 million tons of diesel and gasoline in 2024; assuming a levy of \$0.05/L, the annual revenue raised for the purchase of carbon credits was around \$300 million. Assuming a 10% administration fee and a carbon price of \$30/tCO_2, 10 million tons could be purchased per annum while the direct impact, assuming an elasticity of −0.05 and a fuel price of \$2/L, would be only some 50,000 tCO_2 reduced due to lower fuel consumption.[73] However, KliK Foundation, the carbon offset grouping mechanism for the Swiss fuel importers, needs to use a large share of funds for domestic carbon projects which are prioritized based on the Swiss CO_2 law.[74] For national carbon credits, prices are significantly higher and can reach \$200/tCO_2 or more. It is therefore clear that the GHG impact from the carbon tax on transport fuels is not derived primarily from the lower consumption levels but from using the additional funds to finance activities and projects that reduce carbon emissions.

Carbon prices are included in various countries within the frameworks for making policy decisions. For example, in the EU and the UK, major transport infrastructure projects that benefit from public support must conduct an appraisal that uses a carbon price to estimate the cost of carbon emissions. This means that carbon emissions are integrated into the planning decisions of policymakers. This in turn can be effective in promoting transport projects that reduce GHG emissions. Similar approaches are used by multilateral development banks in their economic appraisal of investments.

4.3. Opportunities in CAREC Countries

As of 2025, CAREC countries do not levy any carbon taxes, although transport fuel taxes with the same impact have been established in most of them. An interesting option could be to combine a carbon tax on fossil transport fuels (gasoline and diesel) with revenues raised used to fund domestic transport emissions reduction projects. This would allow for indirect additional funding of projects relative to their GHG impact and would enable a country to better reach its NDC transport targets. While recycling of carbon taxes is not uncommon, the funds are not used specifically for transport projects and are also not linked in general to carbon markets. Linking carbon taxes to domestic carbon markets can foster low-carbon transport initiatives but has been used little outside Switzerland.[75] Recycled carbon taxes linked with domestic carbon markets have had only a limited impact on the domestic transport sector for the following reasons:

[72] See e.g., Climate Cent Foundation; KliK Foundation; and Federal Office for the Environment (FOEN). Climate.

[73] KliK Foundation, the carbon offset grouping of Swiss motor fuel importers, does not pay a fixed price but has closed for example agreements at this price level.

[74] Federal Assembly of the Swiss Confederation. 2021. Federal Act on the Reduction of CO_2 Emissions.

[75] Switzerland's CO_2 law requires domestic CO_2 reductions and allows for a limited quantity of international credits. The carbon tax is not levied on transport fuels but an agreement has been made with fuel importers that a "voluntary" levy is put on transport fuels, which is recycled to finance domestic and international carbon credits. A significant number of domestic carbon projects are thereby in the transport sector: see Carbonoffset. 2025. Registered Projects in Switzerland. 19 September.

- **The price is too low to effectively promote low-carbon transport activities.** Many domestic carbon markets are linked to a carbon tax that is often established at a very low level of \$5–\$10/tCO_2. At these prices, it cannot be expected that transport mitigation activities will be additional to BAU. For a measurable impact, a minimum price of \$25 is required, while a price beyond \$50 is considered necessary for a significant impact. Switzerland, for instance, pays prices of up to \$250/tCO_2 for its domestic carbon market transport projects.

- **Domestic carbon markets in many countries do not limit offset projects to being domestic.** In some countries, such as Colombia, the carbon tax can be offset with domestic or international projects. This does not foster domestic emissions reductions and results in a large supply of very low-cost projects. If a country wants to reduce domestic transport emissions, it must limit the supply of carbon credits to national projects. While international carbon markets might be globally cost-effective, they will not help countries attain their domestic GHG emissions reduction targets.

- **Most domestic carbon markets are not sectoral but allow for any type of emissions reduction project**.[76] The transport sector has however in most cases higher abatement costs than, e.g., the energy and industry sectors. As measures in the transport sector have a long lead time with assets being used for many years, it is however important to invest at an early stage already in transport projects. It would thus be far more effective to limit offsets from transport projects for a domestic carbon market related to the transport sector.

- **Payments are based on results obtained after implementation of the investment.** In general, carbon markets are results-based finance with payments being received upon delivery of emissions reduction units. Most transport projects are however heavily loaded upfront with capital costs. Carbon credits can in most cases not be transformed to up-front payments or only at a very high discount. Barriers related to up-front payments are due to risks of changing market rules and regulations, e.g., governments not approving more carbon credits or changing rules during the implementation phase, or the risks of buyers not honoring contracts. Carbon markets would have a higher impact if payments could be made, at least to a significant degree, up front. For example, the Swiss domestic e-bus program received a large influx of clients upon establishment of an up-front payment per e-bus of more than \$100,000 equivalent to around 6–7 years of carbon credits.

As discussed in Section 3, the direct GHG impact of fuel price increases is, at least in the short run, very low due to the price inelasticity of fuel demand. A completely different approach is to use the revenue streams resulting from a marginal price increase in fuels to finance the incremental costs of transport mitigation measures. The incremental costs are thereby assumed to be reflected by the cost of high-quality carbon market credits in the transport sector.

[76] See, for example, Colombia; the Republic of Korea; Mexico; South Africa; Switzerland; and British Columbia, Canada.

A domestic transport carbon market could be linked to a very low transport fuel carbon tax with the following potential impact:

- Income source creates the demand for carbon credits. A levy of e.g., $0.01/L of gasoline and diesel sold in a country could be applied. Table 5 shows, based on fuel quantities sold, the resources that could be tapped per CAREC country with such a "climate cent" fund.
- The proceeds of the climate cent fund are used exclusively for domestic carbon credit transport projects. This can be justified as the tax is imposed only on transport fuels and proceeds are thus targeted to the transport sector with the goal of decarbonizing transport.
- The carbon price paid could be based on annual auctions.
- Half of the projected and externally validated emissions reductions over the lifetime of the project are paid up front to allow for up-front investments.
- The management of such a facility could be realized by a private sector entity selected through competitive bidding, reducing political interference and allowing for efficient management of resources. The domestic carbon market could be based on the Verified Carbon Standard (VCS) with a potential methodological flexibility to allow for deviations of approaches or new approaches.

Table 5: Annual Projected Revenue of a Climate Cent Fund per Country

Country	Diesel and Gasoline Sold, 2023 (million L)	Annual Revenues for a Climate Cent Fund ($ million)
Azerbaijan	3,620	36
People's Republic of China	343,222	3,432
Georgia	1,371	14
Kazakhstan	10,641	106
Kyrgyz Republic	394	4
Mongolia	2,309	23
Pakistan	16,911	169
Tajikistan	962	10
Turkmenistan	2,766	28
Uzbekistan	2,813	28

L = liter.
Note: Calculations based on levy of $0.01 per liter of diesel and gasoline sold in the country based on last available year (in general 2023).
Source: International Energy Agency. Energy Statistics Data Browser (accessed 15 October 2025).

Based on an average carbon price of $25 such a fund could reduce 0.2 million–6.8 million tCO_2 per annum (Table 6; excluding the PRC). To clarify, the estimated emissions reductions are not due to the increased fuel price but are a consequence of using proceeds from a fuel price increase to pay for transport mitigation activities, e.g., through a carbon market system. The initial estimates made depend on various assumptions cited above and are more in the sense of an illustration of the potential of such a measure. This could form the basis to achieve domestic carbon emissions targets under the Paris Agreement. Surplus reductions could be sold together with corresponding adjustments to other countries but only at prices that significantly surpass the domestically paid price. This would allow for further growth of the fund.

Table 6: Potential Annual Transport Emissions Reductions from a Climate Cent Fund

Country	Annual Revenue Accruing to Climate Cent Fund ($ million)	Projected Annual Transport Emissions Reductions (million tons of carbon dioxide)	Estimated Transport Mitigation Target per annum in Nationally Determined Contribution (million tCO_2)	Share of Estimated Nationally Determined Contribution Target (%)
Azerbaijan	36	1.4	2.2	65
Georgia	14	0.5	0.6	96
Kazakhstan	106	4.2	2.2	190
Kyrgyz Republic	4	0.2	0.1	235
Mongolia	23	0.9	0.7	126
Pakistan	169	6.8	8.9	76
Tajikistan	10	0.4	0.5	73
Turkmenistan	28	1.1	1.7	66
Uzbekistan	28	1.1	4.6	24

tCO_2 = tons of carbon dioxide.

Notes:

1. Based on 2024 data.
2. The greenhouse gas emissions reductions estimated are not due to a direct impact from increasing the fuel price. The impact is based on using revenues from a marginal increase of fuel prices to finance incremental costs of transport mitigation measures, e.g., through purchase of carbon credits from transport projects.
3. The analysis and figures above are initial estimations based on multiple assumptions and are given for illustrative purposes only.
4. Annual revenues are based on $0.01/L of diesel and gasoline transport fuel tax.
5. Projected annual emissions reductions are based on an average carbon credit price paid of $25 per ton of carbon dioxide.
6. Estimated nationally determined contribution (NDC) transport emissions targets are based on the following:
   - Azerbaijan: No specific transport target in its NDC; the general unconditional 35% reduction target relative to 1990 emissions is thus used; transport emissions of 1990 used as base.
   - Georgia: Specific transport target in its NDC of 15% reduction target relative to 1990 emissions; transport emissions of 1990 used as base.
   - Kazakhstan: No specific transport target in its NDC; the general unconditional 15% reduction target relative to 1990 emissions is thus used; transport emissions of 1990 used as base.
   - Kyrgyz Republic: Based on NDC 3.0 unconditional mitigation target for the transport sector for 2030 (absolute target of 67,000 tO_2 reduction).
   - Kazakhstan: No specific transport target in its NDC; the general unconditional 23% reduction target relative to business-as-usual (BAU) emissions is thus used.
   - Pakistan: No specific transport target in its NDC; the general unconditional 15% reduction target relative to BAU emissions is thus used.
   - Tajikistan: No specific transport target in its NDC; the general unconditional 23% reduction target relative to BAU emissions is thus used.
   - Turkmenistan: No specific transport target in its NDC; the general unconditional 20% reduction target relative to 2010 emissions is thus used; transport emissions of 2010 used as base.
   - Uzbekistan: No specific transport target in its NDC; the general unconditional 35% reduction target relative to 2010 emissions is thus used; transport emissions of 2010 used as base.

Source: Authors.

Such a carbon fund purchasing carbon credits from the transport sector could help countries achieve a substantial share of their transport emission reduction targets under the unconditional NDC commitments. Based on the median across all countries assessed, the fund could support reductions equivalent to around 75% of targeted total transport emissions reductions. Some countries could reduce more than 100% of targets, meaning sales could be made to third parties. The idea of a national carbon fund raising revenue through a minimal carbon tax on transport fuels and used for domestic transport mitigation projects builds upon the successful experience in particular of Switzerland.

Chapter 5

EMISSIONS TRADING SYSTEMS

This chapter reviews how ETSs are used as an instrument in general, their application to the transport sector, and then their application in CAREC countries.

5.1. Emissions Trading System Instrument

In a carbon tax system, the price of emissions is set by policymakers; this price then determines the emissions result that is achieved. Under an ETS, policymakers determine the volume of emissions allowances instead of the price, i.e., it is a quantity-based policy allowing the market to set the price of carbon. An ETS under a cap-and-trade system is managed by a governing jurisdiction that sets a limit (cap) on total emissions for regulated entities covered by the ETS within a given period. The cap ensures that a predetermined emissions outcome is achieved. Emissions allowances are handed out to mandated participants either for free or auctioned. The liable entities need to surrender emissions allowances to the system administrator over a compliance period. Allowances can be traded among market participants and potentially other market actors. The participants can either reduce internally their emissions or purchase allowances from other participants or, if permitted as a means of compliance by the system, by purchasing credits from outside the system. Linking between different ETS can also increase possible options for participants to comply with their allowance target, thereby reducing costs.[77] An ETS under a baseline-and-credit system sets emissions targets (baselines) for regulated entities, which can then earn tradable credits for emissions below their baseline. This approach focuses on performance relative to a baseline.

An ETS can either be a credit or an allowance system. The EU's ETS, for example, trades in allowances. The government first distributes a finite number of allowances to entities covered by the ETS. These allowances can then be traded between entities based on their emissions reductions. In a credit system like California's cap-and-trade, entities that reduce their emissions below the predetermined baseline generate credits, each representing a reduction or removal of 1 tCO_2.

Coverage of the ETS depends on each system. This includes what GHGs are included and what facilities, sectors, or subsectors of the economy are included. Typically, energy-intensive industrial sectors and the power sector are included due to their abatement potential and the (in general)

[77] See for more details ADB. 2015. *Emissions Trading Schemes and Their Linking: Challenges and Opportunities in Asia and the Pacific* and World Bank. 2021. *Emissions Trading in Practice: A Handbook on Design and Implementation*.

large proportion of emissions of these sectors. In many cases liable entities are also related to threshold values, e.g., under the EU's ETS, a thermal input value for combustion plants is fixed with entities exceeding the threshold values obliged to participate in the system. Under some ETS, entities that do not meet the threshold value can opt-in to participate.[78] Individuals and non-regulated entities can also participate indirectly in an ETS by trading allowances for investment or other purposes. The transport sector is included in some ETS, such as California's cap-and-trade system, which includes the transport sector upstream by including fuel suppliers in respect to the emissions associated with the fuel they sell to customers, and the Republic of Korea's ETS, which includes companies emitting more than 125,000 tCO_2 per year and facilities with emissions in excess of 25,000 tCO_2 per year (e.g., KoRail, the operator of the national railway system, participates).[79] The first stage of the EU's ETS included domestic aviation and maritime transport but excluded road-based transport. ETS2, which commences from 2027 onward, will also include road transport, although as a separate system. Fuel suppliers in the road sector will be responsible for buying allowances covering emissions upstream and not at the consumer level (households or vehicle users). Fuel suppliers will be required to surrender allowances to cover their emissions, purchasing these allowances at auctions with the goal of bringing emissions down by 42% by 2030 compared to 2005 levels.[80]

Enforcement measures to ensure compliance generally include financial penalties, which should be significantly higher than the expected allowance cost. Penalties need to be paid in addition to surrendering the missing allowances (e.g., in the next year). Penalties can be a fixed amount (e.g., under the EU's ETS, this is €100/tCO_2 adjusted annually with inflation)[81] or related to the market price of allowances (e.g., as under the Republic of Korea's ETS). Crediting mechanisms or offsets are a flexibility measure allowed by certain ETS. They allow participants to meet their targets by acquiring carbon credits generated by projects in a crediting system outside the scope of an ETS. This again can be, based on the system regulations, from same region (under regional ETS) or national or international projects, and can be linked to certain project types. It is also often linked to a certain percentage maximum of offsets that can be used. Within the Republic of Korea's ETS, for example, carbon credits from transport projects outside the scope of the ETS are used.

ETS can be implemented on a regional (e.g., the EU's ETS), national, or subnational level. As of April 2025, 40 regions, economies, or subnational entities had implemented ETS, with the first being the EU's ETS in 2007. In Asia, national ETS have been established in Indonesia, Kazakhstan (since 2013), the Republic of Korea, and the PRC. Subnational ETS have also been established in the PRC (e.g., Beijing and the Chongqing pilot ETS), as well as Japan's Tokyo and Saitama. As of 2025, India; Japan; Malaysia; Pakistan; the Philippines; the Russian Federation's Sakhalin; Taipei,China; Thailand; Türkiye; Ukraine; and Viet Nam were considering or preparing an ETS.

[78] This is possible for example under the Swiss ETS as this can result in financial incentives due to repayment of the CO_2 tax paid (see FOEN. Climate.)

[79] International Carbon Action Partnership. Korea Emissions Trading System (K-ETS).

[80] European Commission. ETS2: Buildings, Road Transport and Additional Sectors.

[81] European Commission. Monitoring, Reporting, and Verification.

Figure 5: Emissions Trading Systems Compliance Price per Country/Region, 1 April 2025

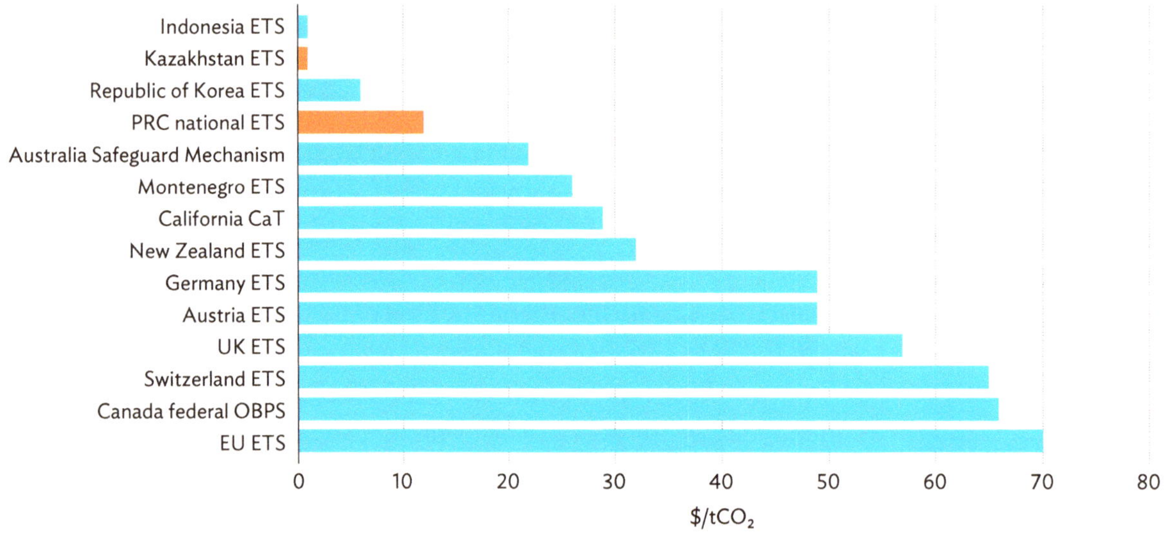

CaT = cap-and-trade, PRC = People's Republic of China, ETS = emissions trading system, EU = European Union, OBPS = output-based pricing system, tCO_2 = tons of carbon dioxide, UK = United Kingdom.
Note: Orange refers to Central Asia Regional Economic Cooperation member countries.
Source: World Bank Group. State and Trends of Carbon Pricing Dashboard (accessed 27 April 2026).

The compliance price rate of ETS varies from $1/tCO₂ in Indonesia to $70/ tCO₂ in Kazakhstan under the EU's ETS (Figure 5).

Under an ETS, a government can create a revenue stream primarily through the sale of CO_2 allowances, in general through auctioning. The EU's ETS auctioning revenues amounted to nearly €44 billion in 2023, of which €33 billion went to member states and the remaining to the Innovation Fund and the Modernisation Fund. The allowance price in 2023 was on average €83/tCO_2. Revenue streams depend of course largely on ETS coverage, the amount of free allowances handed out by the government, and the ETS price (in 2017 the EU's ETS had an allowance price of €5/per tCO_2).[82]

Since June 2023, EU member states have been obliged to use 100% of revenue collected to support specific climate action and energy transformation purposes, except for any revenue that they spend in aid for electricity-intensive industries for indirect carbon costs (previously the rate was 50%).

[82] European Environment Agency. 2025. Use of Auctioning Revenues Generated Under the EU Emissions Trading System.

5.2. The Transport Sector and Emissions Trading Systems

The transport sector can be incorporated into an ETS in various ways, including by assigning allowances directly to transport companies, incorporating transport fuels, or establishing an allowance system for CO_2 emissions of vehicles.

5.2.1. Transport Companies

The transport sector is regulated under some national or regional ETS, such as that of the Republic of Korea, where large emitters, including the rail operator, are included. The major GHG impact of a public transport operator is not their direct GHG emissions but rather the avoided GHG emissions of private modes of transport not regulated within an ETS. If transport operators have absolute emissions targets, increasing their operations would increase direct emissions, hurting them financially, while the indirect GHG impact of reducing overall transport emissions through mode shift is highly positive. The incorporation of public transport operators into an ETS can therefore be problematic.

5.2.2. Inclusion of Transport Fuels in an Emissions Trading System

The inclusion of transport fuels in an ETS is problematic as the price elasticity of transport fuels is limited and a shift toward increasing the use of biofuels can create numerous social and environmental problems, as well as very high upstream GHG emissions related to their production and land-use change-related emissions. Increasing the use of biofuels can also hamper ramping up use of EVs.

California's cap-and-trade system includes fuel distributors emitting more than 25,000 tCO_2 per annum based on their fuel sales (around 30 million L of fuel). Since 2015, fuel distributors of diesel, gasoline, or gaseous fuels must acquire allowances (each allowance is 1 tCO_2) either at quarterly auctions or through trading, i.e., fuel distributors can purchase and sell allowances with other entities within the ETS. The cost of allowances is passed on to consumers in the form of higher fuel prices, which in turn result in lower GHG emissions, albeit with a limited impact due to low demand elasticities. The fuel distributors can also invest in low-carbon fuels, e.g., mixing biogas with fossil gas or biofuel blends of liquid fuels.

At the last auction in August 2025, the allowance price was $29/$tCO_2$, while the price ceiling of allowances as of 2025 was $95.[83] Since 2022, allowance prices have remained roughly constant, fluctuating between $26/$tCO_2$ and $42/$tCO_2$. An allowance price of $29/$tCO_2$ results in a fuel price increase of around $0.08/L. California has very high shares of biofuel compared to other US states, especially in diesel. This is due to the cap-and-trade program and the low-carbon fuel standard and has led to the high usage of non-sustainable biofuels resulting, indirectly, in hampering the deployment of EVs.[84]

83 California Air Resources Board. 2026. California Cap and Invest Program; California Air Resources Board. Price Ceiling Information.
84 J. St. John. 2024. California's Biofuel Bias is Hampering its EV Future. Can that Change? *Canary Media*. 12 March.

5.2.3. Vehicle Carbon Allowances

The EU, US, and other countries have established CO_2 emissions targets or standards for vehicles combined with tradable zero-emission vehicle (ZEV) credits or with pooling of manufacturers or vehicle importers. In the US, manufacturers get credits if their fleet beats the standard. Credits can be averaged across a company's fleet, banked for future years, or traded with other manufacturers. Credits are, therefore, tradable compliance assets or regulatory credits. The EU does not have directly tradable ZEV credits, but pooling and joint compliance are allowed between manufacturers. The noncompliance penalty is €95 per gram of CO_2 per kilometer (gCO_2/km) per car registered above the target, which is fixed annually or for certain periods. Switzerland has a similar system, but with car importers, as the country has no vehicle manufacturers. For CAREC countries without vehicle manufacturers, the Swiss approach could thus be followed, which is essentially the same as the EU system but based on vehicle dealers and importers.

These systems have the following in common:

- They set a clear standard per newly registered vehicle of gCO_2/km based on the type of vehicle's approval test (a standardized test procedure, made once per vehicle type)—the standard needs to be ambitious and below the current average emissions factor of newly registered vehicles to result in a GHG reduction.

- They set a penalty for noncompliance, which needs to be high enough to spur production and/or import of low-carbon vehicles.

- They allow for trading or pooling, which allows, e.g., EV manufacturers to receive additional revenues paid by fossil vehicle manufacturers or dealers. The additional revenues are used to make EV manufacturing more profitable or reduce EV prices, thus boosting EV sales.

This is a market-based, efficient system to foster the registration of new low-carbon vehicles. It can be applied to all newly registered vehicles, new or used. However, it does not apply to the sale of secondhand cars within a country, i.e., vehicles already registered. This allows customers the choice of purchasing high GHG-emitting vehicles at higher prices or to get an EV, which indirectly receives a subsidy from high-emitting vehicle manufacturers. EU standards for average CO_2 emissions from new cars have pushed companies toward developing electric and low-emissions vehicles. While public demand for these cars is not always high, it can be increased by reducing prices.

Car manufacturers pool to meet the EU's Corporate Average Fuel Economy standards. For example, Ford, Mazda, Stellantis, Subaru, and Toyota have teamed up with Tesla to pool their carbon emissions. Meanwhile, Mercedes has partnered with Polestar, Volvo Cars, and Smart. By pooling with Tesla, automakers can reduce their average emissions and avoid paying hundreds of millions of euros in penalties.[85] Automakers such as Tesla and Polestar, whose sales are 100% electric, can sell their

[85] Jennifer L. 2025. EU's 2025 Emission Rules Led Tesla and Mercedes to Pool Carbon Credits to Avoid $15.6 Billion Fine. *Carbon Credits.* 20 January.

surplus carbon credits to other manufacturers pooling with them. Figure 6 shows the income earned by Tesla from the sale of carbon credits. Continued demand for carbon credits (also called regulatory credits in this context) suggests that this revenue stream will remain relevant as long as traditional automakers need to comply with emissions standards. Tesla's leading position in the EV market ensures a steady supply of credits for sale.

Figure 6: Tesla's Regulatory Credits Revenue

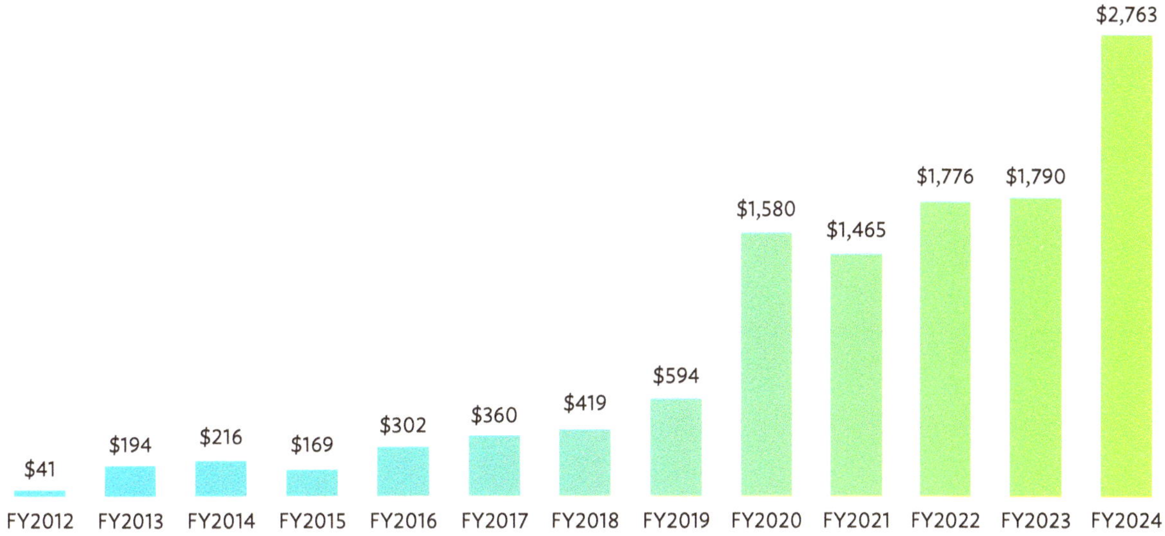

FY = fiscal year (ending 31 December).
Source: StockDividendScreener.com. 2026. Tesla Regulatory Credits: Revenue, Credit Sales Per Car, and Profit Margin Impact. 28 April.

While absolute revenue figures have grown for Tesla, the share of revenues generated by credits dropped over time from around 10% in 2012 to around 2% in 2025 (Figure 7).

Emissions pooling in Europe, therefore, significantly impacts EV sales by creating financial incentives for car manufacturers to increase their EV production and sales. Automakers are simultaneously investing in new EV technologies to reduce reliance on carbon credits in the long term. For instance, Stellantis has emphasized its focus on innovative electric and low-emissions technologies, ensuring compliance while minimizing costs. As more automakers invest in EVs, the reliance on pooling agreements may diminish. However, until that transition is complete, carbon credits will remain a critical tool for compliance. The impact on EV prices is shown in Figure 8, which indicates the revenue per car sale of Tesla from carbon credits.

Each EV sold in 2024 earned $1,500 of "subsidy" while high-emitting fossil fuel cars must pay this cost. Such systems thus apply the polluter-pays principle and leave freedom to choose to customers. They are an effective means to achieve significant GHG reductions of the transport sector in a technology-neutral manner.

Figure 7: Tesla's Regulatory Credits to Total Revenue Ratio

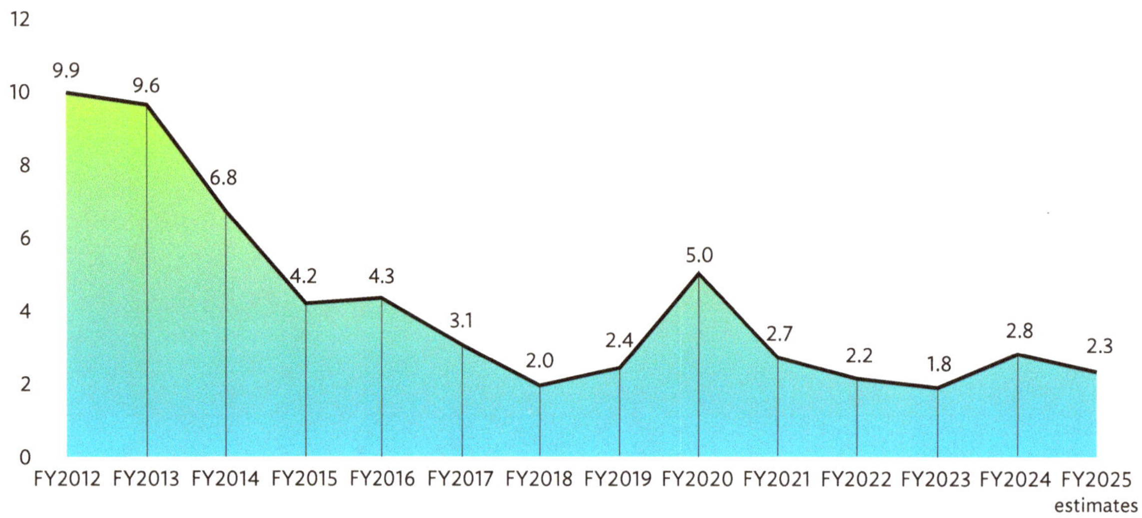

FY = fiscal year (ending 31 December).
Source: StockDividendScreener.com. 2026. Tesla Regulatory Credits: Revenue, Credit Sales Per Car, and Profit Margin Impact. 28 April.

Figure 8: Tesla's Regulatory Credits per Car

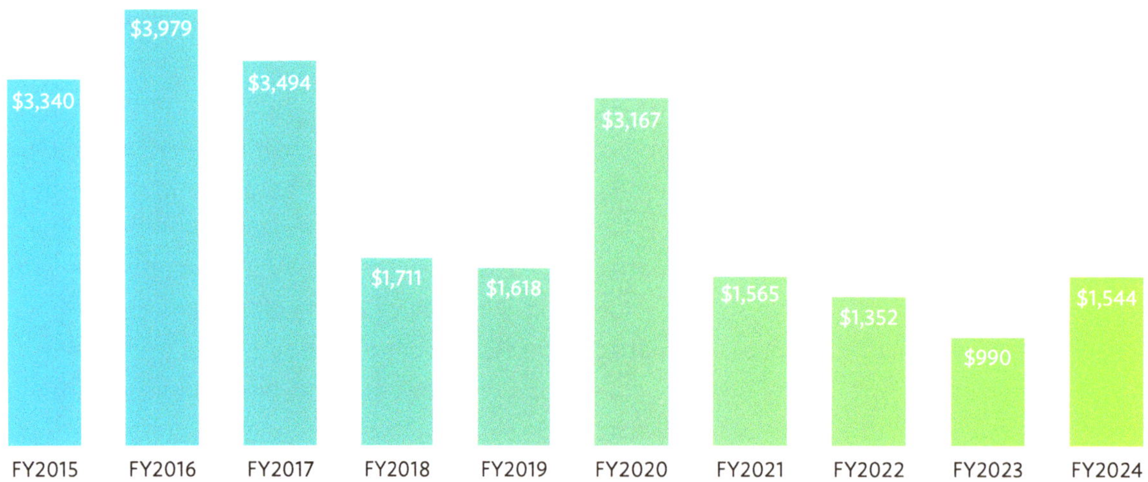

FY = fiscal year (ending 31 December).
Source: StockDividendScreener.com. 2026. Tesla Regulatory Credits: Revenue, Credit Sales Per Car, and Profit Margin Impact. 28 April.

5.3. Opportunities in CAREC Countries

Within CAREC countries, only the PRC and Kazakhstan have established ETS. The national ETS of the PRC covers electricity, heat, and the industrial sectors.[86] Kazakhstan's ETS covers electricity, heat, industry, and the mining and extractives sectors.

The transport sector has two distinct features compared to the energy and industry sectors that should be considered when establishing an ETS incorporating the transport sector:

(i) Emissions sources are atomized (i.e., are a very large number of individual entities) and relatively small (i.e., have very low emissions per individual entity). Most emissions from the transport sector come from individual vehicle owners and not from large logistics, rail, or public transport companies. This makes their insertion into an ETS difficult. Inclusion of fuel suppliers, as done in California, is of limited use to reduce GHG emissions as fuel suppliers do not decide on vehicles purchased. It has a certain impact rather on increasing the share of biofuels.

(ii) Public transport companies, rail, and shipping companies have their main impact through enabling a mode shift away from road to rail or from individual mobility to public transport, i.e., they have a positive impact on the emissions of third parties and not the entity itself. Regulating emissions of the entity itself, i.e., the public transport, rail, or shipping companies, could result in increasing the costs of their services and reducing service levels, thus resulting in a reduced mode shift.

A high impact potential would be to establish CO_2 emissions targets or standards for vehicles combined with tradable ZEV credits or with pooling of manufacturers. If well designed, this results in a reduction of GHG emissions of the transport sector and encourages the use of technologies and production of vehicles with low- or zero-carbon emissions. It is an especially useful instrument to target the atomized individual vehicle market and has been successful in pushing EVs without involving large government subsidies. CAREC countries mostly use European vehicle emissions standards, which could be linked with CO_2 vehicle emission standards establishing for each country its own path of decrease. As most countries have no or only a limited vehicle industry, an ETS with tradable permits for CO_2 vehicle emissions would need to be tied to vehicle importers and dealers, comparable to the structure as used in Switzerland.

[86] Some subnational ETS in the PRC included the transport sector, e.g., the Beijing pilot ETS.

Chapter 6

CARBON MARKETS

This chapter reviews carbon markets as an instrument, then looks at their application to the transport sector, and their application in CAREC countries.

6.1. Carbon Market Overview

Carbon markets are systems where carbon credits that reduce or remove GHG emissions are traded. Their ultimate aim is to reduce GHG emissions in a cost-effective manner. In terms of geographic scope, carbon markets can be subnational, national, regional, or international. There are two types: Compliance markets created through laws and regulations implemented by regional or national governments that are mandatory for participants, and voluntary markets where participants set their own goals to meet voluntary commitments. Both types of markets use carbon credits generated from activities that reduce or remove GHGs according to specified rules and requirements set by carbon standards. In voluntary markets, participants have no formal obligations and set their own goals to meet voluntary commitments while in compliance markets the goals are established by governments or international treaties in a mandatory manner.

In terms of geographic scope, carbon markets can be subnational, national, regional or international.

ETS create compliance markets through governments setting a cap and companies trading allowances. In many cases an ETS allows for carbon credits from outside the system to be used at least partially as allowance. However, compliance carbon markets can also be realized without an ETS and can be linked for example to a carbon tax, e.g., the South African Crediting Mechanism or the Colombian Crediting Mechanism.

A crediting mechanism is related to project or program-based activities that comply with specific standards of registries or involved entities. Carbon credits can be used to meet compliance under national or international agreements, domestic policies, or corporate citizenship objectives related to GHG mitigation.[87]

[87] World Bank. Climate Countdown: Carbon Pricing.

Fundamental markets to which carbon credits cater and that have differences in terms of access conditions, prices, and transaction costs include

- domestic carbon credit markets (voluntary and compliance),
- voluntary international carbon markets, and
- international compliance markets under bilateral or multilateral schemes.

Procedures for all carbon markets are very similar, involving a methodology to be eligible for project activities and a process of stakeholder consultation and project documentation, followed by an external validation and registration at the standard (Figure 9). The procedure is repeated during project implementation, involving annual monitoring reports that follow the methodology and project documentation, as well as external verification and a review at the standard before carbon credits are issued. Typically, the time required for project formulation is 3–6 months; validation is also 3–6 months, and registry is another 3–6 months.

Figure 9: Process Flow of a Carbon Credit Project

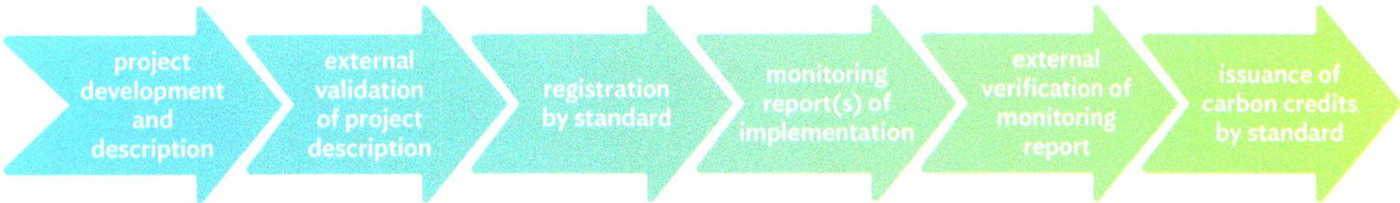

Source: Authors.

Carbon credits are a form of results-based finance. Payment is usually based on the delivery of the carbon credits. The amount received is not based on a projection in project documentation, but rather on actual, externally verified results. Up-front payment based on projections is, in general, not possible or only with very high discounts. This means in practical terms that between the start of development of a project and the first disbursement, a period of 2–3 years is normal. Credits can be received in general for 10 years or the maximum lifespan of the equipment, whichever comes first. For Paris Agreement Crediting Mechanism (PACM) projects, however, contracts in general only go to 2030, as no post-Paris Agreement deal has yet been negotiated.

National Carbon Markets

National compliance carbon markets are established to meet domestic GHG targets in a cost-effective manner and are established in conjunction with an ETS or a carbon tax or a hybrid system. National voluntary carbon markets are created to reduce GHG emissions in a cost-effective manner with the aim of channeling funds into national emissions reduction activities that go beyond compliance goals.

Domestic carbon markets can be at local, regional, or national levels. National or subnational carbon markets have been established in more than 30 countries, mostly in conjunction with an ETS, where offsets can be used at least partially instead of allowances, or in systems with a carbon or environmental tax, where carbon credits can be used (Boxes 3 and 4). In some cases, the carbon credits that can be used are limited to those originating in the region or country, while in others, local carbon credits compete with international carbon credits. Carbon credits might also be limited to specific project types. Standards used are local, national, or international, such as the Clean Development Mechanism (CDM) standards of the United Nations Framework Convention on Climate Change (UNFCCC) or voluntary carbon market standards, e.g., Verified Carbon Standard (VCS) or Gold Standard. Prices vary greatly. If related to a carbon tax, the carbon credits are traded at a discount relative to the tax; the same holds if related to a penalty in case of not surrendering sufficient units in an ETS.

Box 3: Thai National Voluntary Carbon Market

The Thailand voluntary emissions reduction program (T-VER) was created in 2013 and implemented in 2014 by the Thailand Greenhouse Gas Management Organization (TGO) as a domestic greenhouse gas (GHG) crediting mechanism to support the voluntary reduction of GHG emissions and promote a domestic carbon market.[a] Carbon credits known as TVERs can be used for carbon offsetting of companies, individuals, events, and so on. TGO establishes the rules and regulations under which the market operates, publishes methodologies that can be used for T-VER projects, and approves projects. T-VER Methodologies are largely based on Clean Development Mechanism methodologies. By 2024, approximately 170 projects had been certified with an emissions reduction volume of 1.5 million tons of carbon dioxide (tCO_2). In 2023, sales prices ranged from $1.50/$tCO_2$ for renewable energy projects to $8/$tCO_2$, with the highest price fetched by forestry and land use projects. Many credits are unsold in the registry, indicating an oversupply and weak demand.

To increase prices and demand, TGO developed the Premium T-VER standard aligned with the requirements of Article 6 of the Paris Agreement, with the goal being to sell carbon credits into the Paris Agreement compliance market.[b] Rules concerning inter alia additionality, baseline determination, and project start dates differ also differ to T-VER.[c] Premium-TVER credits can, e.g., be used under the Carbon Offsetting and Reduction Scheme for International Aviation scheme, but T-VER units cannot.[d]

Additionally, TGO is assessing the option of linking carbon credits with the ETS and the carbon tax Thailand is planning, which would effectively move at least some credits to a domestic compliance market. The experience of the Thai domestic voluntary market of a limited appetite and low price for such credits is not uncommon—Costa Rica for example experienced similar issues with its domestic carbon market.[d]

[a] TGO is an autonomous public organization operating under the supervision of the Ministry of Natural Resources and Environment and under the authority of the Government of Thailand.
[b] TGO. 2025. *2024 Thailand's Voluntary Carbon Market Updates Report*. (In Thai.)
[c] TGO. 2025. *Guideline for Premium Thailand Voluntary Emission Reduction Program*.
[d] International Civil Aviation Organisation (ICAO). *ICAO Expands Approved Emissions Unit Programmes for Effective CORSIA Implementation*.
[e] World Bank. 2020. *The Costa Rican Offset Mechanism (MCCR)*.

Source: Compiled by authors.

Box 4: South Africa's Carbon Credit Market

The South African Crediting Mechanism was introduced 2019 and has recently undergone reforms. A core aspect is that national carbon credits can be used as offset allowance which allows a taxpayer to reduce the amount of carbon tax payable by using carbon offsets. As of 2025, the maximum reduction level as a total of greenhouse gas emissions was 10% for combustion emissions, with an increase expected to 15% by 2026. Project activities that can generate an offset and procedures to follow are defined in the national carbon offset regulations. The Ministry of Finance approves the standards that projects must follow. These are the Clean Development Mechanism, the Verified Carbon Standard, or the Gold Standard. The Carbon Offsets Administration System acts as a registry. South African carbon credits typically trade at a 10% to 25% discount to the carbon tax rate. The carbon tax rate in South Africa is around $14 and shall increase to $27 by 2030. As of November 2025, the Carbon Offsets Administration System had 45 registered projects with 22 million tons of carbon dioxide of carbon credits listed and 21.6 million tons retired.

Source: Compiled by authors.

Voluntary International Carbon Markets

In a voluntary carbon market, private actors voluntarily buy and sell carbon credits (reductions or removals). The market is not regulated by governments. The purpose of the voluntary carbon markets is the same as for compliance markets: GHG reductions achieved in a cost-effective manner. Commitments of private actors that can result in the purchase of carbon credits include corporate net-zero targets and other voluntary climate or environmental claims. The voluntary market allows private capital to flow into GHG emissions reduction activities. Typically project owners or project developers develop a carbon credit project under the regulations of the chosen standard, all of which have similar principles and procedures (Figure 11). Carbon credits generated by registered projects are then sold directly or through platforms or brokers to buyers using the carbon credits to offset their own emissions or to contribute toward global GHG reductions.[88]

The voluntary carbon market saw a sharp decline in volumes and values (prices multiplied by volumes) in 2023 and a continued decline in 2024. However, the voluntary carbon market is also characterized by very large price differences between types of projects. Prices range from less than $\$1/tCO_2$ to over $\$100/tCO_2$, with an average of $\$6/tCO_2$ in 2024—prices depending on the project type, its attributes, size, sustainable development benefits, and marketing appeal, among other factors.[89] Integrity of carbon credits in the voluntary market has been a key concern and is being addressed by stakeholders such as the Integrity Council for the Voluntary Carbon Market. Demand has also dropped from companies who have been criticized for purchasing carbon credits or for claiming zero-carbon products and services. It is thus unclear if prices and volumes in the voluntary carbon market will continue to fall, eventually remaining with some low cost credits plus some "high integrity" credits or if the market will move more toward compliance-type credits, which can

88 Offsetting implies compensating emissions the buyer of the credits has emitted, while contribution emphasizes the support for climate action.

89 See World Bank. 2025. *State and Trends of Carbon Pricing*; Ecosystem Marketplace. 2025. *State of the Voluntary Carbon Market 2025*; and Carbon Credits. Live Carbon Prices Today.

Figure 10: Volumes and Prices of Voluntary Carbon Markets, 2020–2024

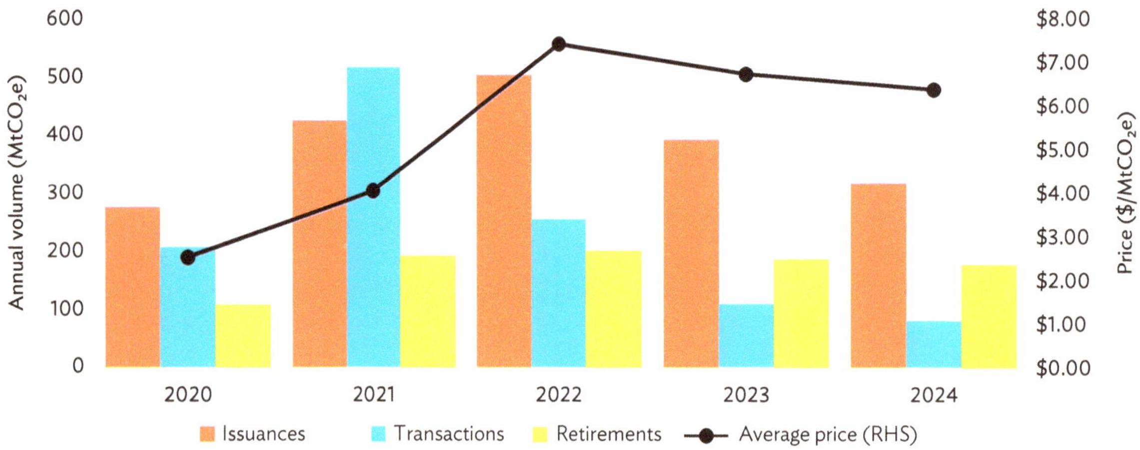

$MtCO_2e$ = million tons of carbon dioxide equivalent, RHS = right-hand side.
Source: Ecosystem Marketplace. 2025. *State of the Voluntary Carbon Market 2025*.

also be used by entities and persons for voluntary purposes but with fewer issues related to double claiming or double counting, and potentially fewer fears from buyers concerning the integrity of the carbon credits.

Multiple carbon market standards exist, the most used by far being VCS, then the Gold Standard. All types of sectors are included in voluntary carbon markets, including removals. As of 2025, nature-based removals and clean-cooking projects were the most popular project type in terms of volumes transacted in the voluntary market. The transport sector has registered some projects in voluntary carbon markets, but overall participation is limited (Section 4.3) due to various reasons, including:

- Mode shift projects have complex methodologies and require considerable data collection to establish baselines, as well as significant monitoring efforts, including regular costly passenger surveys. Data required for baseline determination, including fuel consumption of different vehicle categories per fuel type, vehicle occupation data, and trip distance data, are all in general not available at city level—vehicle registration statistics do not even include at the national level in most countries a disaggregation of fuel type and even less so for cities. New public transport systems are important for maintaining or even increasing ridership levels and to provide a convenient, safe, and attractive transport option. However, they are not necessarily more efficient than existing public transport systems and they might only result in a very limited mode shift from private means of transport. The acclaimed lighthouse project bus rapid transit (BRT) of TransMilenio in Bogota, Colombia for example was the first registered CDM transport project. The carbon market project developed and monitored by Grutter Consulting [authors of this report] showed limited mode shift and, especially after the expansion of services to the Integrated Public Transport System (Sistema Integrado de Transporte Público or SITP) starting end-2012, emissions per passenger-km of the new BRT system were comparable to the previous bus system.[90] The real impact of the BRT is that with the old system, passengers were moving away from public transport. However, this is difficult to prove and capture under a carbon credit methodology and the UNFCCC never accepted a methodological approach based on worsening baseline emission levels.

- Projects that lead to more efficient logistics and save trips are extremely difficult to capture methodology-wise. No methodologies forwarded in this context under the CDM or voluntary standards have been approved by the UNFCCC.

- Biofuel projects, popular prior to EVs, are extremely difficult to capture from methodological and monitoring viewpoints due to indirect land-use change and leakage impacts. Not surprisingly while some CDM methodologies are available for biofuels (e.g., ACM0017 or AMS-III.T developed by Grutter Consulting) no project has issued carbon credits using these methodologies.

A further issue is also that until recent years, most activities in the transport sector were directed toward reducing air pollutants, with vehicle emission standards for example targeting a reducation in critical pollutants such as carbon monoxide, nitrous oxides, and particulate matter, while the fuel efficiency of vehicles and their CO_2 emissions did not commensurately improve.[91] EVs have surged only recently as an option to reduce massively GHG emissions. For EV projects as well as partially for charging infrastructure, carbon market methodologies exist and their complexity is also limited. Thus, e-mobility especially opens the market for transport projects in the carbon market. This is reflected in a recent surge of such projects in the voluntary carbon market.

International Compliance Markets

International compliance markets include those previously operated under the CDM of the Kyoto Protocol, the new international compliance market under Articles 6.2 and 6.4. of the Paris Agreement, and Carbon Offsetting and Reduction Scheme for International Aviation (CORSIA) managed by the International Civil Aviation Organization.

CORSIA requires covered airlines to offset the growth in their CO_2 emissions beyond 2019 levels by purchasing carbon credits issued by approved crediting mechanisms and eligible units (Box 5).

90 Grutter Consulting managed data monitoring and the carbon credit project for TransMilenio from 2006 to 2015.

91 Euro 0 and Euro V buses and trucks have the same fuel efficiency and CO_2 emissions—see e.g., European Environmental Agency, Computer Program to Calculate Emissions from Road Transport (COPERT) model; private passenger cars have become more efficient engine-wise, but at the same time vehicle weight and power has increased, offsetting these improvements.

Box 5: Overview of the Carbon Offsetting and Reduction Scheme for International Aviation

Member states of the International Civil Aviation Organization (ICAO) adopted the Carbon Offsetting and Reduction Scheme for International Aviation (CORSIA) in 2016, aiming to achieve carbon-neutral growth for the international aviation sector not covered under Kyoto Protocol nor the Paris Agreement.[a] CORSIA only applies to international flights as national flights are covered by the Paris Agreement. CORSIA's baseline is set at 85% of 2019 emissions from 2024 until the end of the scheme in 2035. Compliance periods for airline operators are set for 3-year periods, after which they must demonstrate that they have canceled the appropriate number of emissions units with eligible offsets.

CORSIA had an initial pilot voluntary phase from 2021 to 2023, a second voluntary phase from 2024 to 2026, and a mandatory phase starting in 2027. During the two initial phases, CORSIA only applies to international flights from countries that have volunteered to participate. As of July 2025, 130 countries including the United States (US) were participating voluntarily.[b] Some large countries such as Brazil, India, and the People's Republic of China are not (yet) participating. Participating CAREC countries are Afghanistan, Azerbaijan, Georgia, and Kazakhstan. From 2027, CORSIA will cover all international flights except for least developed countries, small island developing states, and countries with a very small share of international traffic.

Offset obligations shift in the three mandatory phases between 2027 and 2035 from being based on average carbon dioxide growth of the sector toward being increasingly tied to individual operator growth. In 2018, ICAO adopted detailed monitoring, reporting, and verification requirements and rules for aircraft operators, which report their emissions to their national authority. The ICAO Council periodically approves a list of programs that can supply CORSIA Eligible Emissions Units to be used for compliance. CORSIA does not itself register and approve projects but uses well-accepted certification standards such as the Global Carbon Council, the Verified Carbon Standard, or the Gold Standard. CORSIA also defines the standard and the scope of eligibility.

One important additional certification required by CORSIA is that carbon credits must have been authorized by the host country for use in CORSIA to avoid double claiming and for which a corresponding adjustment has been applied. CORSIA also excludes for standards certain project types or methodologies (e.g., large-scale [>15 megawatt] grid-connected renewable electricity generation projects). Eligible carbon credit occurrence dates started on 1 January 2021 with activities that started their first crediting period after 1 January 2016.[c]

[a] Aviation Benefits Beyond Borders. CORSIA Explained; ICAO. Carbon Offsetting and Reduction Scheme for International Aviation (CORSIA); and International Air Transport Association. CORSIA Fact Sheet.

[b] ICAO. 2025. *CORSIA States for Chapter 3 State Pairs*. The US may decide not to implement CORSIA, though as of 2026 US airlines are in favor the scheme, which is only compulsory from 2027. US-sourced credits however might not comply with CORSIA eligibility criteria in terms of corresponding adjustments and no double counting.

[c] ICAO. 2024. *CORSIA Eligible Emissions Units*.

Source: Compiled by authors.

The demand for credits for CORSIA is estimated to be very large, but demand projections are very uncertain.[92] Enforcement of CORSIA obligations on airlines falls on national governments. Therefore, demand materialization depends on domestic legal frameworks, which as of 1 April 2025 have only started to be established in Brazil, Canada, the EU, and the UK. Carbon credits within CORSIA require a corresponding adjustment from the national or host government where credits are generated. Many countries do not yet have the mechanism in place for issuing corresponding adjustments, and some have reported not being willing to issue them.

[92] World Bank. 2025. *State and Trends of Carbon Pricing 2025*.

Like aviation, the international maritime sector does not form part of the Paris Agreement, with the International Maritime Organization (IMO) leading efforts to establish a framework for reducing GHG emissions from shipping, which might eventually result in another compliance market. The IMO Net-Zero Framework combines mandatory emissions limits and GHG pricing across the maritime sector. The Marine Environment Protection Committee of the IMO approved the framework in April 2025; however, its formal adoption did not occur in October 2025 as expected but was postponed to 2026.[93] As of 2025, carbon market methodologies for the shipping sector were available at the Gold Standard and a new methodology for e-fuels in shipping should be published soon at the VCS.

The Paris Agreement aims to limit the increase in global average temperatures to below 2° C and pursue efforts to limit the increase to 1.5° C above pre-industrial levels (Box 6).

Article 6 of the Paris Agreement allows parties to voluntarily cooperate to achieve their emissions reduction (mitigation) targets set out in their nationally determined contributions (NDCs). Article 6.2 is based on voluntary agreements between cooperating countries. A centralized international trading mechanism called the Paris Agreement Crediting Mechanism (PACM) was established under Article 6.4, but it is not yet fully operational. The PACM builds upon and uses similar but updated mechanisms, procedures, tools, and methodologies as the CDM under the Kyoto Protocol. Article 6.2 allows agreements to be tailored by the cooperating countries, while Article 6.4 is centrally regulated by the Article 6.4 Supervisory Body under the PACM.

Box 6: Overview of the Paris Agreement

The Paris Agreement, adopted in 2015, is a legally binding international treaty on climate change requiring each signatory nation to set its own emissions reduction target.[a] These are set out in countries' nationally determined contributions (NDCs) submitted every 5 years. In 2025, the NDC 3.0 was required to be submitted—as of mid-November 2025, 119 countries had done so, including Azerbaijan, the People's Republic of China, the Kyrgyz Republic, Mongolia, Pakistan, and Uzbekistan. The Paris Agreement allows party countries to meet or outperform these targets through international cooperation, or the trade of internationally transferred mitigation outcomes. A country's NDC includes a section on how it intends to use the market mechanism under Article 6 of the Paris Agreement and describes the actions it will take to mitigate greenhouse gas emissions and implement adaptation. The Paris Agreement reaffirms that developed countries should take the lead in providing for climate finance to support developing countries in mitigation and adaptation efforts. Countries need to report transparently on actions taken and progress achieved under the enhanced transparency framework, which includes submitting, since 2024, regular biennial transparence reports reviewed by technical experts to ensure accountability and build trust.

[a] United Nations Climate Change. The Paris Agreement.
Source: Compiled by authors.

[93] IMO. The IMO Net-Zero Framework—FAQs.

As of 2025, Article 6.2. buyers were Australia, Japan, the Republic of Korea, Kuwait, Liechtenstein, Monaco, Norway, Singapore, Sweden, Switzerland, and the United Arab Emirates, with Japan, the Republic of Korea, Sweden, Singapore, and Switzerland being the most active.[94] Bilateral agreements involving more than 100 host countries have been signed. As of November 2025, host countries with Article 6.2 project activities included Cambodia, Chile, Dominica, Ghana, Kenya, Malawi, Morocco, Peru, Senegal, Thailand, Uruguay, Uzbekistan, and Vanuatu—with Ghana being by far the most active country. Electric mobility had the largest number of projects as of 2025. Of the CAREC countries, only Uzbekistan has a project listed, for landfill gas with the Republic of Korea (the project is not yet authorized).

The first ITMO deal and the first ITMO transfer were structured between Switzerland and Thailand for an e-bus project in 2023 (Box 7).[95]

Box 7: Thai-Swiss e-Bus Project

The Bangkok e-bus project owned by Energy Absolute Company Ltd received the first internationally transferred mitigation outcomes (ITMOs) under the Paris Agreement's Article 6.2 at end-2023. The program includes the deployment of approximately 2,000 electric buses operated by Thai Smile and the operation of some new bus routes. Emissions reductions are achieved due to technology change from gaseous and diesel buses toward electric units and mode shift related to the new bus routes and the additional passengers carried.

The project is fully implemented. It was structured under the bilateral agreement for Article 6.2 projects between Switzerland and Thailand and using methodologies approved by the Thailand Greenhouse Gas Management Organization (at the time of project registration, only standard methodologies were available and not the premium methodologies used for Article 6 projects in Thailand, as of 2025). The ITMOs are traded at an unit price of $40 per ton of carbon dioxide with an offtake agreement until 2030. The buyer of the carbon credits is the KliK foundation of Switzerland, which purchases ITMOs based on an agreement between the foundation and

continued on next page

[94] For an informal list of Article 6 projects from UNEP, see UNEP. Article 6 Carbon Market Cooperation.

[95] KliK. 2024. *Greenhouse Gas Mitigation Activity "Bangkok E-Bus Programme" Delivers First ITMOs Under Article 6.2 of the Paris Agreement for NDC Use*. 8 January.

Box 7 *continued*

Government of Switzerland. The project from the start was limited to private bus operators as the electrification of the public bus operator is considered an unconditional contribution of the Government of Thailand toward its nationally determined contribution target.

A risk analysis study commissioned in 2025 by the Federal Office for the Environment, Government of Switzerland, found moderate to high additionality risks and potential overestimations of modal shift, which affect earlier projections but not actual issued credits.[a] The project has received some criticisms related to infringement of worker rights from the project owner which has stalled at least momentarily ITMO issuance.

Thailand in the meantime has adjusted its regulations concerning Article 6 projects, based on a United Nations Framework Convention on Climate Change (UNFCCC) technical expert review report of Article 6.2.[c] Electric urban buses in general are now also no longer considered as eligible for ITMOs. As of 2025, an Article 6.2 program under the Swiss–Thai agreement for electric trucks, light commercial vehicles, and buses (excluding urban public transport buses) was undergoing authorization, and another project for e-trucks is under validation.

a See Carbon offset implementation CO_2 Compensation or KliK. (Authors of this paper are the owner of the e-mobility program for multiple vehicle categories currently under registration.)
b BeZero Carbon. 2025. *Final Ex Ante Risk Assessment Report Bangkok e-bus Program.*
c UNFCCC. *Report on the Technical Expert Review Under Article 6, Paragraph 2, of the Paris Agreement of the Initial Report Referred to in Chapter IV.A (Initial Report) of the Annex to Decision 2/CMA.3 of Thailand.*
Source: Compiled by authors.

The owners of ITMO projects are generally private entities. ITMO projects include transport projects (Section 4) and are traded at prices between \$25 and \$50/tCO_2.[96] Corresponding adjustments might come with a price tag—e.g., Ghana charges the project \$5/tCO_2 for issuing one.[97]

Revenues from Carbon Markets

With carbon markets, the government revenue stream is more limited. Essentially, carbon market projects are either private sector projects or run by a government corporation (e.g., rail projects). Carbon market projects create an influx of climate finance which helps a country to achieve climate targets, as for example outlined in their NDC. Under the Paris Agreement, governments need to ensure that they do not oversell emissions reductions, i.e., that they only allow for international carbon trading with corresponding adjustments for carbon credits that go beyond the unconditional NDC target of the country. This can best be ensured by creating a positive list of project types that can receive corresponding adjustments or a negative list of projects that cannot receive them. As an example, the Government of Chile excluded urban electric public transport buses and taxis which are cofinanced by the government, and which are included under the unconditional target of Chile within its NDC, from emissions trading under Article 6.2, receiving the approval as ITMOs or receiving corresponding adjustments.

96 Price based on authors' Article 6.2 projects. See also FOEN terms of reference for development of Article 6.2 projects issued December 2025 (file reference: BAFU-061.6-04.32-03-2/1/1) with an indicative maximum price of CHF35/tCO_2 or TCAF with \$30; World Bank. 2023. *Project Appraisal Document on a Proposed Grant in the Amount of US\$46.25 million to the Republic of Uzbekistan for the Innovative Carbon Resource Application for Energy Transition Project*. para. 44.

97 Ghana Environment Protection Authority. 2023. Fees.

A direct revenue stream is obtained if the government charges fees for project authorizations or registration, and/or for issued carbon credits or for corresponding adjustments. The country can also opt to keep a share of the carbon credits for its own purposes, either to comply with its unconditional NDC commitment, or market the reductions on its own. Thailand, for example, keeps 10% of emissions reductions issued by Article 6.2 carbon credit projects cumulatively by 2030. Ghana meanwhile asks for $5 per carbon credit issued with a corresponding adjustment. This fee is used to cover administrative costs of managing the scheme and for a mitigation ambition fund which will finance additional mitigation activities in the country.[98] Kenya has a similar fee structure, asking for $4 per corresponding $0.10–$0.20/tCO_2 issued.[99] Some countries such as Chile and Uruguay do not have any charge on carbon credits. Zimbabwe, at the other extreme, originally asked for 50% of proceeds, which was then reduced in 2023 to 30%. Asking for a high share of proceeds results in two problems:

- Carbon credits are under international competition. Asking for a much higher share of proceeds or higher fees on carbon credits will limit the attractiveness of the country for investments in carbon credit projects. Clients will not be willing to pay a higher price from a specific country and project developers and investors compete for the sale of carbon credits from diverse countries.

- Fewer resources go to the actual project which reduces GHG emissions, making fewer projects financially viable. The higher the proceeds or fees asked for by governments the "cheaper" the emission action or project must be, i.e., the focus will be on low-hanging fruit and projects that are potentially BAU and non-additional, as these have no or a very low incremental cost.

While it is understood that administrative costs need to be recovered, levying a tax on carbon credits reduces potentially the scope for projects. Instead of taxing the source of GHG emissions (e.g., fossil fuels) a tax is levied on projects which mitigate GHG emissions. This is not considered to be a useful approach for cost-effective GHG mitigation.

6.2. Carbon Market Transport Projects

This section looks at the application of carbon market projects in the transport sector. Transport projects can also supply carbon credits to systems based on carbon taxes or ETS. Examples are:

The Colombian carbon market is linked to a carbon tax of around $6/t$CO_2$. Entities that need to pay the carbon tax can offset part of the payment with carbon credits, which are typically traded with a discount of 20% or more relative to the carbon tax. For example, the registered CDM transport project for cable cars in Medellin sold carbon credits generated after 2012 to the petroleum corporation with a 20% discount.[100]

[98] Government of Ghana. 2022. *Ghana's Framework on International Carbon Markets and Non-Market Approaches*.

[99] GIZ. 2025. *Review of Economic and Non-Economic Instruments to Foster Article 6 Contributions to NDC Achievement in Host Countries*.

[100] Prior to 2012, the project had an international buyer with a significantly higher price but after the collapse of international carbon market prices post-2012 this was no longer an option.

- The Republic of Korea's ETS allows for the usage of domestic and international credits linked with Korean companies. The registered Korean project for high-speed rail (HSR) sold in the initial years into the Korean market but was then stopped by national authorities due to concerns of double counting, as transport entities with significant GHG emissions are also part of the ETS.[101] The ETS also includes the national railway company and aviation companies. While the project reduces emissions of the non-included road transport sector through modal shift, this concept was not understood until recently by national authorities, showing the complexity of transport credits in an ETS that also includes transport companies.

- In the Swiss domestic market, a CO_2 tax was established for non-transport fuels. For transport fuels, an agreement between fuel importers and the government was reached not to establish a carbon tax on transport fuels but to levy a "voluntary" "climate-cent" by fuel importers on gasoline and diesel sold as transport fuel. The petroleum association established a foundation to manage this income, purchasing domestic and international carbon credits that were then surrendered to the government. The government defines the amount of national and international credits that must be surrendered within a given period and approves each project. This created a market for domestic carbon credit projects, not only from the transport sector.[102] Multiple domestic transport projects, including e-buses, e-trucks, e-vessels, e-mobile machinery, hydrogen vehicles, biofuels, and mode shift from road to rail, have been registered and are selling carbon credits for up to \$200/tCO_2 to the foundation.

The section reviews at the global level transport projects registered or under discussion in different types of carbon markets, the procedures and costs involved to participate in them, and what type of transport projects match best with carbon markets as structured today.

6.2.1. United Nations Framework Convention on Climate Change and the Clean Development Mechanism

The CDM market, the first compliance carbon market, has been replaced by the PACM. Any project registered under the CDM (or part of the voluntary market) had to use an approved methodology eligible to the project type. CDM methodologies can in general also be used by the standards in the voluntary market, serving at least as reference for Article 6.2 projects, and are used as a base for the methodologies to be approved under Article 6.4. Therefore, while the CDM itself is no longer operational, the instruments developed under its auspices, including tools, methodologies, MRV approaches, and documentation of projects, remains highly relevant and is the basis for many methodologies within domestic and voluntary market standards as well as for the PACM.

[101] For registration as a project, the methodology as well as the project document needs national approval and monitoring needs to be nationally verified and undertake a cumbersome national approval process.

[102] For a list of registered projects see FOEN. Climate.

Methodologies for the following types of transport projects were approved under the CDM:[103]

- implementation of mass rapid transit systems (e.g., metro, LRT, BRT);
- cable cars for passenger transport;
- electric and hybrid vehicles;
- modal shift of road to rail or shipping (note that the two methodologies in this area are not well formulated and very difficult to apply, which has resulted in no projects yet receiving carbon credits using them);
- HSR;
- production of biofuels;
- usage of specific devices to increase vehicle efficiency, e.g., idle-stop or retrofit devices;
- biogas, hydrogen, or liquefied natural gas usage;
- efficient vehicle fleets (note that this methodology too is hardly applicable due to severe applicability limitations and excessive monitoring requirements and has not been used by any project);
- shore-side electricity for vessels (cold-ironing); and
- lightweight two-/three-wheelers.

The CDM also has two specific tools relevant for transport projects: (i) baseline emissions for modal shift measures in inter-urban cargo transport, and (ii) baseline emissions for modal shift measures in urban passenger transport.[104]

Some methodologies have proven to be too complex or onerous to be applied in practice, including those for modal shift of road to rail or shipping and biofuel; neither projects nor monitoring reports requesting issuance of carbon credits have been forwarded for these methodologies. The best applicable methodologies are those for mass transit systems, HSR, and EVs.

Nearly 8,000 projects and programs were registered under the CDM, of which only 30 were transport-related. Of these, more than half did not enter monitoring reports and did not receive carbon credits, even though they had successfully registered the project.[105] Table 7 shows the types of transport projects registered under the CDM.

[103] See for approved large-scale methodologies: UNFCCC. Approved Baseline and Monitoring Methodologies for Large Scale CDM Project Activities; and for approved small-scale methodologies, UNFCCC. Approved SSC Methodologies.

[104] UNFCCC. Tools.

[105] This is largely due to the collapse of the price for CDM emissions reduction certificates after 2012, making monitoring of the projects financially nonviable.

Table 7: Registered CDM Transport Projects, as of end-2025

Project Type	No. of Registered Projects	Host
Mass transit (bus rapid transit, light-rail transit, metro, cable car)	20	People's Republic of China, Colombia, Guatemala, India, Tunisia
Electric vehicles	4	India
Others	6	People's Republic of China, India, Malaysia, Paraguay

CDM = Clean Development Mechanism.
Source: Compiled by authors using UNFCCC. Activity Search (accessed 15 October 2025).

Most registered transport projects were for mass transit. India had the most transport projects (10), followed by Colombia (6), Mexico (5), and the PRC (5). From CAREC countries, only the PRC has registered transport projects under the CDM.

6.2.2. Voluntary Carbon Market Standards

Voluntary carbon market standards for mitigation projects include the VCS (with a registry of around 2,500 projects), the Gold Standard (4,400 registered projects) and the Global Carbon Council (around 1,000 projects). VCS-approved transport methodologies include those from the CDM, plus six others, including most prominently one for EV charging systems, plus one for electric mobile machinery, and one for alternate fuels (e-fuels) for shipping (under publication).[106] Table 8 shows active transport projects within the VCS.

Table 8: Active Verified Carbon Standard Transport Projects, end-2025

Project Type	No. of Projects	Economy
Electric mobility	48	Bangladesh; Brazil; Chile; People's Republic of China (PRC); Iceland; India; Kenya; Republic of Korea; Malaysia; Mexico; Morocco; Nigeria; Pakistan; Singapore; South Africa; Taipei,China; Thailand; Togo; Türkiye; United Arab Emirates; United States; Viet Nam
Mass transit	2	PRC
Others	6	PRC, India, Thailand, United Kingdom

Note: Active is defined as either registered and having made issuances in the last 5 years, under validation, or under listing for not more than 2 years.
Source: Compiled by authors based on Verified Carbon Standard (accessed 15 October 2025).

Under the VCS, 56 projects are active, with most being EV projects. Transport projects no longer active included various mass transit projects as well as other project types. Projects are well distributed over the globe. From CAREC countries, the PRC and Pakistan have active VCS transport projects as of February 2026. The year until May 2026 has seen a surge of new electric mobility programs seeking validation or registration.

[106] VERRA. VCS Program Methodologies.

Gold Standard-approved transport methodologies include those from the CDM, plus four other methodologies, including one for two- and three-wheelers and three from the shipping sector (for efficiency improvements of vessels, not for fuel switch nor mode-shift).[107] Table 9 shows the types of active transport projects listed by the Gold Standard.

Table 9: Active Gold Standard Transport Projects, end-2025

Project Type	No. of Projects	Country
Shipping	13	International, People's Republic of China, Greece, United States
Electric mobility	4	Kenya, New Zealand, Senegal
Others	3	India, Republic of Korea, Switzerland

Note: Active is defined as either registered and having made issuances in the last 5 years, under validation, or under listing for not more than 2 years.
Source: Compiled by authors based on Gold Standard Impact Registry. Projects (accessed 15 October 2025).

The Gold Standard has 20 active planned or registered transport projects, most of which are international shipping retrofit and international shipping advanced hull-coating projects. Of CAREC countries, the PRC has one listed project.

The Global Carbon Council has two listed metro projects from India, one not very relevant approved transport methodology (for carpooling), and an EV charging infrastructure methodology under development.[108]

6.2.3. Domestic Carbon Markets

The following are local carbon markets that include multiple transport projects.

The Australian Carbon Credit Unit Scheme (ACCU) currently includes 13 transport projects (excluding revoked ones).[109] This includes vehicle replacement projects, EV projects, and efficient vessels and fleets. Only two projects so far have received carbon credits. The scheme closed the land, sea, and transport method by 31 March 2025, so no further new projects are possible from the transport sector.[110] The original transport method aimed to improve fuel efficiency and included activities such as biofuel usage, efficient tyres, and optimizing vehicle schedules.[111]

The Swiss domestic carbon market system started at the end of the 1990s with voluntary agreements where the GHG emissions impact was determined based on governmentally approved individual project or program methodologies, and results were monitored based on standardized

[107] Gold Standard for the Global Goals. Transport.

[108] Global Carbon Council. Submitted for Global Stakeholder Consultation (accessed 15 October 2025); Global Carbon Council. Methodology Development.

[109] Government of Australia, Clean Energy Regulator. ACCU Project and Contract Register (accessed 15 October 2025).

[110] Government of Australia, Clean Energy Regulator. Land and Sea Transport Method (closed).

[111] Government of Australia, Ministry of the Environment. 2015. Carbon Credits (Carbon Farming Initiative— Land and Sea Transport) Methodology Determination 2015.

protocols. At that stage, more than 100 transport companies operating trucks and building machines participated, reducing GHG emissions with biofuels, efficient logistics, mode shift of road to rail and road to shipping, low-carbon vehicles, and other measures. Since then, the market has evolved to domestic carbon credits with multiple registered transport projects, including road-to-rail mode shift projects, electric and hydrogen vehicles (trucks, buses, vessels, and mobile machinery), increase of tyre pressure, and biofuels.[112] Swiss domestic prices paid for transport projects can be up to $\$200/tCO_2$. The carbon projects are financed through a levy established on fossil transport fuels by the fuel importers based on an agreement with the Government of Switzerland, with the foundation managing the program delivering an agreed-upon quantity of domestic and international carbon credits to avoid a transport fuel carbon tax.

Other countries with domestic market crediting schemes include Thailand, with the Thailand Greenhouse Gas Management Organization overseeing around 300 active projects, of which five are for electric mobility and three are biofuel projects, Japan (J-Credits), and various provinces in Canada and Mexico.[113]

6.2.4. International Compliance Markets Under the Paris Agreement

Article 6.2. Projects

Article 6.2. projects are based on bilateral agreements between countries, with around 100 bilateral agreements in place between 61 different countries (Table 10 shows those involving CAREC countries). A total of 160 pilot projects have been recorded, of which 133 are overseen by Japan's Joint Crediting Mechanism (JCM) (Box 8).

Table 10: Bilateral Article 6.2 Agreements and Projects with CAREC Countries, end-2025

CAREC Country	Country Agreements Made With
Georgia	Japan, Switzerland
Kazakhstan	Japan, Republic of Korea
Kyrgyz Republic	Japan
Mongolia	Japan, Republic of Korea
Uzbekistan	Japan

CAREC = Central Asia Regional Economic Cooperation.
Source: United Nation Environment Programme. Article 6 Carbon Market Cooperation (accessed 11 November 2025).

112 FOEN. Climate.
113 Thailand Carbon Credit Registry.

Box 8: Japan Joint Crediting Mechanism

The Joint Crediting Mechanism (JCM) is administered by the Government of Japan. JCM bilateral agreements were closed with 31 countries as of August 2025 covering 268 registered projects, 11 of which are in Mongolia. Only three small transport projects have been registered by the JCM, covering mode shift road to shipping, compressed natural gas–diesel buses, and eco-drive.[a] The JCM projects must involve Japanese technologies, products, systems, services, or infrastructure. JCM has numerous published methodologies (JCM projects need to use JCM-approved methodologies) for the transport sector for efficiency improvements of vehicles, for electric vehicles, and natural gas-powered vehicles including vessels, and for fuel-cell electric vehicles.[b]

[a] Global Environment Center Foundation. List of JCM Financing Programme by MOEJ (FY2013–2024) as of 24 July 2025.
[b] J-Credit Scheme. Methodologies.
Source: Compiled by authors.

Table 11 shows Article 6.2. transport projects under development or authorized.

Table 11: Article 6.2 Transport Projects, end-2025

Project Type	No. of Projects	Countries
Electric mobility	12	Cambodia, Chile, Dominica, Ghana, Peru, Senegal, Thailand, Uruguay
Others	3	Indonesia, Viet Nam

Note: Includes Joint Crediting Mechanism projects.
Source: Compiled by authors, based on United Nations Environment Programme data and KliK.

E-mobility is by far the most popular project type. This can be based on one category or one project participant (e.g., the Thai e-bus program with Energy Absolute or a program in Ghana for electric bicycles) or it can be multi-vehicle type (e.g., programs in Dominica, Chile, Uruguay, Peru and one in Thailand). The program in Dominica includes for instance all vehicle categories as well as electric vessels, public charging infrastructure, and solar photovoltaic electricity generation for vehicle charging.

Article 6.4 Projects

The Article 6.4. rules agreed at the Conference of the Parties 26 allow for the transition of CDM projects to the Article 6.4 mechanism, contingent upon host country approval (deadline end-2025), receiving corresponding adjustments, meeting additional design activity requirements, and meeting the crediting period of end-2025. It is currently unclear how many projects will receive host country approval and comply with the established rules. The PACM manages a list of prior considerations with some 1,100 projects and programs. Table 12 shows Article 6.4 prior considerations for CAREC countries.

Table 12: Prior Consideration for Article 6.4 Projects in CAREC Countries, November 2025

Country	No. of Projects	Transport Projects
Azerbaijan	3	0
PRC	3	1 EV project
Georgia	1	1 EV project
Kazakhstan	3	0
Kyrgyz Republic	0	0
Mongolia	2	0
Pakistan	23	2 EV projects
Tajikistan	0	0
Turkmenistan	0	0
Uzbekistan	8	1 EV project

CAREC = Central Asia Regional Economic Cooperation, PRC = People's Republic of China, EV = electric vehicle.
Source: Compiled by authors based on the United Nations Framework Convention on Climate Change. Prior Consideration Notifications (accessed 25 October 2025).

The PACM market is not yet operational. Various core aspects and methodological tools have already been approved including tools on "common practice analysis" and "investment analysis." However, only one methodology, for flaring or use of landfill gas, has been approved to date. The 2026 preliminary workplan of the supervisory body includes the approval of core standards such as a standard for setting baselines in mechanism methodologies and a standard for demonstration of additionality.[114] The workplan does not include the revision of any CDM transport methodology in 2026. It is thus questionable that Article 6.4 will be operational for transport projects in 2026.

6.2.5. Comparison Markets and Project Types

Table 13 shows the pros and cons of different carbon markets relating to transport projects.

Table 13: Carbon Markets and Transport Projects

Item	Complexity	Price Paid	Major Challenge
Domestic market	Depends on country	In general low	A framework for the domestic market needs to be in place
Voluntary market	Moderate	Low (<$10)	Low price, limited and diminishing demand
CORSIA	Moderate	Medium to high ($20–$25 with potential increase in future)	Requires corresponding adjustments from the government, and thus a framework in place and approval from the government
Article 6.2	High	High ($25–$50 with potential increase)	Approval of the host and buyer governments is required, and a framework needs to be in place
Article 6.4	High	Medium to high[a]	Approval of the host government, a framework needs to be in place, and the PACM needs to be operational including approved transport methodologies

CORSIA = Carbon Offsetting and Reduction Scheme for International Aviation, PACM = Paris Agreement Crediting Mechanism.
[a] Expected to be at least at CORSIA level and presumably comparable to Article 6.2 deals.
Source: Based on conversations of authors with carbon market brokers.

[114] UNFCCC. Methodologies.

The minimum project size is heavily dependent on prices being paid, as transaction costs (payments for validators and verifiers) and project documentation costs are size-independent. For an electric mobility program or project (being the most popular transport project type) typical costs for project development and external validation up to registration are approximately $100,000 per project. Annual monitoring and verification expenses up to issuance are for the same project type in the order of at least $50,000. Mass transit projects have significantly higher development costs as they require data collection surveys per site and also incur far higher monitoring costs (again related to data collection costs, including regular passenger surveys). Mass transit projects also suffer from a high insecurity of actual emissions reductions due to problematic passenger forecast projections of mass transit system developers and high uncertainty related to mode-shift and trip distances.

Table 14 rates the most popular transport project types (based on registered project types as well as listed NDC transport mitigation activities in CAREC countries) relative to the core criteria carbon market projects need to fulfill.

It is not surprising that most proposed transport projects are related to electric mobility in 2025. Not only is this considered key to decarbonization of the transport sector and the area with the largest mitigation potential, but tools and procedures are available to develop such projects with a reasonable cost.

Table 14: Transport Project Types Versus Critical Criteria for Carbon Market Projects

Project Type	Methodology Availability/Complexity	Monitoring Complexity	Development and Monitoring Costs	Project Size	Lead Time Till Operations
Biofuels	Available but very complex	Very high complexity	Very high monitoring costs	Small to very large	Short (can be less than 1 year) with large volumes from the start
Mass transit systems	Available but complex	High complexity	Very high development and monitoring costs	Medium to large	Time for construction of systems can be years; volumes grow but are significant from start
Electric mobility	Available and relatively simple	Low to medium	Moderate costs	Micro to very large[a]	Short but gradual build up
Rail projects	Available tools but no useful methodology outside high-speed rail	Low to medium	Moderate to high development and monitoring costs	Medium	Time for construction of can be years; volumes grow but are significant from start

[a] Stand-alone projects, e.g., electric bicycles, are on the micro-scale while grouped projects with charging infrastructure and multiple EV categories can be very large.

Source: Compiled by authors.

6.3. Options for CAREC Countries

Carbon credit projects can be designed for the national or the international market. Internationally the most promising markets are the CORSIA and the PACM. Following are options that CAREC countries are considering or implementing for transport projects.

6.3.1. Azerbaijan

Azerbaijan highlights the importance of environmentally friendly transport and especially public transport in its updated NDC. It has implemented various policies promoting EVs, while electrification of railway lines is planned, and new electric passenger trains and locomotives for cargo transportation have been acquired.

Electric Vehicles

Within the framework of Conference of the Parties 29 as a pilot project, 160 electric buses were delivered and deployed on Baku city routes; further 3,000 electric buses are set to be deployed in Azerbaijan.[115] To access international carbon markets, critical benchmark figures must be below a certain threshold for electric mobility projects. If these threshold levels are surpassed, EVs and charging infrastructure are considered BAU and projects in this area cannot be considered for carbon markets.[116] The UNFCCC methodology for EVs (AMS-III.C) uses as its threshold level EV sales of less than 2.5% of overall sales per vehicle category for the average of the last 3 years.[117] For charging infrastructure projects, the VCS methodology has a benchmark of 5% of EVs being in the corresponding vehicle stock over the last available year. In both cases, Azerbaijan is still below these threshold values, but EV growth can be explosive as the examples of Nepal, Thailand, and Viet Nam show.

The GHG impact of EVs depends to a significant extent on the carbon grid factor. Azerbaijan has a grid factor of 384 gCO_2 per kilowatt hour, based on the carbon grid factor for electricity usage used by international financial institutions (IFIs), which is on par with world average. Table 15 shows estimated GHG emissions reduction per annum per vehicle category that can be claimed through a carbon market project, based on the carbon grid factor of Azerbaijan and standard mileages and energy consumption figures per vehicle category.

---

115 Press Service of the President of the Republic of Azerbaijan. 2024. Ilham Aliyev Got Acquainted with Activities of Zigh Electric Bus Depot. 31 October; and Sustainable Bus E-Magazine. 2024. 3,000 E-Buses are Coming to Azerbaijan, According to Government's Plan. 3 May.

116 Exceptions apply potentially for bilateral carbon deals, which follow bilaterally agreed-upon criteria and approaches, and for national carbon markets.

117 Theoretically if financial additionality is proven the sales level can be higher.

Table 15: Azerbaijan's Estimated Greenhouse Gas Emissions Reduction Impact per Vehicle Category per Annum

Vehicle Category	Greenhouse Gas Reduction per Annum (tons of carbon dioxide)
Urban bus	51
Intercity bus	33
Passenger car	2.5
Taxi	5
Light commercial vehicle for urban deliveries	7
40-ton truck	50

Source: Authors' calculations.

A project with 3,000 electric urban buses could thus achieve an annual emissions reduction of around 153,000 tCO_2 with annual financial benefits from the sale of carbon credits worth \$4 million–\$5 million.

The recommended approach would be to have a general e-mobility carbon credit program for the country, including various EV categories as well as charging infrastructure. Azerbaijan had by 2021 more than 1.3 million passenger cars and more than 160,000 trucks with very high vehicle growth rates.[118] Assuming that by 2030 3,000 electric urban buses are circulating, 1% of trucks are electrified, and 5% of passenger cars are electric and consuming 30% of their electricity at charge points, a program could generate theoretically by 2030 around 600,000 tCO_2 reductions, worth around \$18 million.

Metro Expansion

In 2017, the Baku metro network covered 37 km with a ridership of over 222 million passengers annually. There are plans to expand Baku metro (Azerbaijan NDCs specifically mention the "development of metro transport and increase of a number of metro stations"). Delhi's metro is the most experienced and longest carbon market project related to metros, having gained carbon credits since 2021.[119] Based on monitored Delhi metro data and using the carbon grid factor of Azerbaijan, each metro passenger reduces GHG emissions by around 700 gCO_2. An additional 100 million passengers would thus generate annual emissions reductions of 70,000 tCO_2. With the presentUNFCCC methodology for mass transit projects, Baku metro would be eligible. However, such projects are complex to develop and monitor, and would require an annual minimum size of at least 50,000 tCO_2 reduced, even with high carbon prices of more than \$30 /tCO_2, to warrant the involved complexities and transaction costs.

118 Statista.com. Total Number of Road Motor Vehicles in Azerbaijan in Selected Years, by Type (accessed November 2025).
119 UNFCCC. Project 4463: Metro Delhi, India.

Railway Expansion

As of 2019, Azerbaijan's rail network comprised 2,140 km of operational lines, with 1,169 km already electrified. Azerbaijan recently purchased 50 electric locomotives, with 40 intended for freight transport. Rail transportation contributed 15 million tons of goods and close to 4 million passengers carried in 2019.[120] The Azerbaijan Railway Company has undertaken several decarbonization actions, including railway electrification, published its first sustainability report in 2024, and has prepared, with the support of ADB, a decarbonization policy and framework. The company seeks to develop a corporate-level carbon trading desk aligned with international carbon market mechanisms to monetize carbon credits and contribute to global emissions reduction goals, and is supported in this endeavor by ADB.

The potential for emissions reductions is in electrification of the rail. Electrification itself is not expected to have a very large impact as modern diesel trains are very efficient. The major impact would be from mode shift for freight and passenger traffic. The GHG impact will largely depend on the number of passengers and amount of cargo transported and the average trip distance. GHG emissions of a train per passenger-km are typically 3–5 times lower than for intercity buses and 3–7 times times lower per ton-km (t-km) for rail transport compared to road transport (dependent on cargo type). Thus, a rail system can result in large GHG reductions. However, no international carbon market methodology has been developed yet to support mode shift of any rail systems excluding high-speed rail (HSR).[121] A transport methodology (for freight as well as for passenger transport) would need to be developed first to register a railway project. Such a methodology could be entered under the VCS and subsequently be used by railway projects worldwide.

6.3.2. People's Republic of China

The PRC's updated NDC includes measures to foster low-carbon transport, e.g., with stronger public transport and NMT, mode shift to rail and water transportation for passenger and freight transport, low-carbon fuels, and fostering EVs. The PRC has multiple provincial ESTs and carbon markets to which projects could potentially cater. Provincial ESTs and provincial carbon markets define their own mechanisms and eligibility criteria and as such all types of transport projects could be potentially eligible. Using international standards however (UNFCCC, VCS), various transport project types may no longer be eligible due to them being common practice.

[120] Asian Transport Observatory. 2024. *Transport and Climate Profile: Azerbaijan*. ADB.

[121] The approved UNFCCC freight methodology AM0090 has applicability conditions such as only transport of one cargo type, and identical origin-destinations for all cargo over the lifespan of the project, which are impractical.

Electric Mobility

In 2024, the EV stock share of passenger cars in the PRC was 11%. The share for vans was 5.8%, for buses 30%, and for motorcycles 39%.[122] Around 74% of urban public transport buses were electric.[123] These shares surpass the threshold value of 5% fixed for being eligible for charging infrastructure projects for these vehicle categories. Projects for dedicated charging infrastructure for trucks (stock share 1.2%) would still be eligible. No EV-vehicle project for any road category would be eligible as all vehicle categories have surpassed the 2.5% sales share benchmark for the last 3 years. Electric mobile machinery, e.g., for ports, airports, the construction industry, or the mining sector, would still be eligible.

Using international standards, any carbon market electric mobility project would have to focus on charging infrastructure for trucks and/or on the deployment of electric mobile machinery.

Public Transport

Carbon market projects in this area could use the approved UNFCCC methodology ACM0016. The methodology has a process incorporated to determine whether the proposed project activity is common practice in the host city where the project activity is intended to be implemented. If the city already has a share of 20% or more of public transport trips realized on the same public transport category as the proposed project activity, it is considered common practice and non-eligible as carbon market project. Public transport categories are differentiated into metro, suburban rail, LRT including trams, autonomous-rail rapid transit, BRT, and conventional bus systems. In many cities, metros and BRT are probably common practice (and conventional bus systems in most, if not all). Autonomous-rail rapid transit is not common and in a considerable number of cities LRT systems, metros, and BRT probably also not. The PRC has experience with various registered CDM public transport projects, which issued carbon credits more than a decade ago. New investments in expanding public transport systems could again be attractive to create carbon credits. However, such projects are complex to develop and monitor and require at least annual reductions of 200,000–300,000 tCO_2, with average carbon prices of \$5–\$10 paid as of 2025 in provincial carbon markets. Projects of this size require considerable public transport investments to attract annual additional ridership of approximately 400 million passengers.

Mode Shift of Road to Rail and Road to Water

The PRC has an extensive network of HSR. UNFCCC methodology AM0101 is used for HSR, which has been applied e.g., in the Republic of Korea's Honam HSR line constructed by KoRail.[124] The methodology however has an applicability criterion that less than 20% of rail trips in the country are made by HSR (baseline scenario). In 2024, over 75% of rail trips were made by HSR in the PRC, i.e., the threshold value of 20% has already been well surpassed.[125]

[122] International Energy Agency. Global EV Data Explorer (accessed 14 April 2026).
[123] Government of the PRC. 2024. *Urban Passenger Transport Development Report*.
[124] UNFCCC. *Large-Scale Methodology: High Speed Passenger Rail Systems*.
[125] *Xinhua*. China's High-Speed Railways Offer Majority of Passenger Trips in 2024. 16 January.

Nevertheless, the construction of new rail lines or of increasing water-based transport, especially for freight, can have a major impact on mode shift and result in significant GHG emissions reductions. GHG emissions of a train per passenger km are typically three to five times lower than for intercity buses and 3–7 times lower per t-km for rail transport compared to road transport, dependent on the cargo type. However, no international carbon market methodology has been developed yet to support mode shift of any rail systems excluding HSR. A transport methodology (for freight as well as for passenger transport) would need to be developed first to register a railway project. Such a methodology could be entered under the VCS and subsequently be used by railway projects worldwide.

6.3.3. Georgia

Georgia is developing an integrated National Energy and Climate Plan to identify 2030 targets and consistent policies for reducing GHG emissions across sectors, including transport. The plan includes measures like tax incentives for electric and hybrid vehicles and improved public transportation energy efficiency. It also outlines targets for the share of electric and hybrid vehicles in the registered fleet: 10% electric and 40% hybrid by 2030, increasing to 35% electric and 60% hybrid by 2050. Georgia has as unconditional commitment in its NDC to reduce GHG emissions by 35% below the 1990 level by 2030, with the transport sector aiming to reduce GHG emissions by 15% relative to the reference level by 2030.

Electric Vehicles

Approximately 9,000 EVs were registered in Georgia as of the end of 2024. In 2003, the country had 1.44 million cars, 118,000 trucks including light commercial vehicles, 54,000 buses, and 70,000 other vehicles, meaning the share of EVs was around 0.5%.[126] Tbilisi largely replaced old diesel buses with compressed natural gas (CNG) units, which do not result in GHG reductions. The recent replacement results in a lock-in for the next decade with a fossil solution. Under a European Bank for Reconstruction and Development–Green Climate Fund project, Batumi has received eight electric buses.

To access international carbon markets, Georgia is for all vehicle categories below the threshold values considered as common practice and can thus potentially register EV projects. Based on the carbon grid factor for electricity usage used by IFIs, Georgia has a low carbon grid factor of 135 gCO_2/kWh. Table 16 shows the estimated GHG reduction per annum per vehicle that could be claimed with a carbon market project, based on the carbon grid factor of Georgia and standard mileages and energy consumption figures per vehicle category.

[126] National Statistics Office of Georgia. 2024. *Statistical Yearbook of Georgia 2024*.

Table 16: Estimated Greenhouse Gas Reduction Impact per Vehicle Category per Annum for Georgia

Vehicle Category	Greenhouse Gas Emissions Reduction per Annum (tons of carbon dioxide)
Urban bus	67
Intercity bus	66
Passenger car	3
Taxi	7
Light commercial vehicle for urban deliveries	9
40-ton truck	85

Source: Authors' calculations.

Assuming the NDC target of 10% EVs for all vehicle categories by 2030 and that passenger cars consume 30% of their electricity at charge points, a program could theoretically generate by 2030 more than 1 million tCO_2 reductions, with corresponding revenues of around $30 million. Georgia is interested in Article 6 Paris Agreement markets and already has agreements with Switzerland and Japan for bilateral projects. However, an EV program achieving a 10% target would, at least for passenger cars, hardly be considered as additional, as this target has been formulated in the context of the NDC as an unconditional contribution. This would therefore be a considerable hurdle for any international carbon market project which requires corresponding adjustments.

Public Transport

A pre-feasibility study for network restructuring within the Tbilisi's Green Transport Policy Plan aims to increase bus ridership. Tbilisi's metro system is undergoing modernization with support of the European Bank for Reconstruction and Development, the Green Climate Fund, ADB, and the Asian Infrastructure Investment Bank. Projects that foster increased public transport ridership could qualify for carbon market projects. Here too however, this is a specific target of the NDC and may eventually be included in the sectoral transport target as an unconditional contribution.

6.3.4. Kazakhstan

Kazakhstan's NDC aims to unconditionally reduce 15% of GHG emissions by 2030 relative to the 1990 baseline. As a long-term goal, Kazakhstan aims to achieve carbon neutrality by 2060. The country has integrated sustainable transport development goals into its national strategies, aiming to increase its share of electric and hybrid vehicles to 30% by 2030.

Electric Mobility

Kazakhstan had 13,000 registered EVs as of 1 December 2024. As of 1 February 2025, there were 12,700 electric cars, 350 electric trucks, and 200 electric buses registered. In total, the country has 5.1 million registered passenger cars, 570,000 trucks and 120,000 buses. To access international carbon markets, Kazakhstan is for all vehicle categories below the threshold values considered as common practice and can thus potentially register EV projects. Based on the IFIs, Kazakhstan has a relatively high carbon grid factor of 532 gCO_2/kWh. Table 17 shows estimated GHG emissions reduction per annum per vehicle that could be claimed through a carbon market project, based on the carbon grid factor of Kazakhstan and standard mileages and energy consumption figures per vehicle category.

Table 17: Estimated Greenhouse Gas Emissions Reduction Impact per Vehicle Category per Annum for Kazakhstan

Vehicle Category	Greenhouse Gas Emissions Reduction per Annum (tons of carbon dioxide)
Urban bus	41
Intercity bus	14
Passenger car	1.8
Taxi	4
Light commercial vehicle for urban deliveries	6
40-ton truck	28

Source: Authors' calculations.

Assuming a target of 10% EVs for all vehicle categories by 2030 and that passenger cars consume 30% of their electricity at charge points, a program could theoretically generate by 2030 more than 1.4 million tCO_2 reductions, with revenues of more than $50 million. The recommended approach would be to have a general e-mobility carbon credit program for the country, including various EV categories as well as charging infrastructure.

Railways

Two railway projects are underway connecting Central Asia and the PRC with Europe under the Belt and Road Initiative. The Almaty Railway Bypass Project, which includes the construction of a 130 km electrified railway line specifically designed to enhance cargo transportation along the Middle Corridor and the Dostyk-Moiynty Railway, another Belt and Road Initiative project expected to facilitate high-volume trade and logistics between the PRC and Central Asia.[127] The project will increase freight volumes but no figures are available for additional t-km and type of freight to be transported as of 2025. Calculations on a possible GHG impact are therefore not yet possible. GHG emissions of a train per t-km are typically three to seven times lower per t-km compared to road transport (dependent on cargo type). However, no international carbon market methodology has been developed yet to support mode shift of any rail systems excluding HSR. A transport methodology (for freight as well as for passenger transport) would need to be developed first into register a railway project. Such a methodology could be entered under the VCS and subsequently be used by railway projects worldwide.

[127] Multilateral Investment Guarantee Agency. 2025. Almaty Railway Bypass Project; and B. Kazhibekova. 2025. *Chinese Electric Vehicles (EVs) in Kazakhstan: Public Perceptions and Economic Implications*. (Thesis). University of Turku.

6.3.5. Kyrgyz Republic

The Government of the Kyrgyz Republic's National Development Strategy for 2018–2040 declares the transition to environmentally friendly modes of transport as a top policy priority, specifically including "electrifying municipal and rail transport" as an infrastructure priority.

The Kyrgyz Republic's unconditional targets in its NDC 3.0 provide for a reduction of net GHG emissions by 18% from the projected baseline level of net emissions by 2030 and by 16% from the projected baseline level of net GHG emissions by 2035 (footnote 57). By 2050, the Kyrgyz Republic's goal is carbon neutrality. The updated package of measures in the transport sector includes expanding the use of low-emissions and alternative modes of transport, development of cycling infrastructure, and introducing intelligent traffic management systems (ITMS). Conditional measures include the increase of CNG-powered vehicles and a feasibility study for introducing a fuel tax (10% for gasoline and 4% for diesel). These two measures shall reduce transport emissions relative to the baseline by 67,000 tCO_2 by 2030. As conditional measures, the NDC pledges an increase of EVs (annually increasing the share of EVs by 1 percentage point), micromobility measures, cycling infrastructure, and ITMS. Assessing the implementation result of the NDC2, the NDC3 states that the Kyrgyz Republic has close to 7,000 EVs, representing 60% of the 2025 target of 10,800 units EVs.

Electric Mobility

The Kyrgyz Republic ended 2025 with around 15,000 EVs and, through an ADB project, 120 e-buses. The country had 1.8 million vehicles, comprising 1.4 million passenger cars, 300,000 trucks, and 70,000 buses.

The UNFCCC methodology for EVs (AMS-III.C; the same levels are applied by the corresponding VCS methodology) uses as threshold levels for eligibility as carbon project less than 2.5% of EV sales per vehicle category on average over the past 3 years.[128] For charging infrastructure projects, the VCS methodology used has a benchmark of 5% of EVs in the corresponding vehicle stock in the last available year. To access international carbon markets, the Kyrgyz Republic is for all vehicle categories below threshold values to be eligible for a carbon credit project. Based on the IFIs, the Kyrgyz Republic has a low carbon grid factor of 98 gCO_2/kWh. Table 18 shows the estimated GHG emissions reduction per annum per vehicle class, which could be claimed with a carbon market project, based on the carbon grid factor of the Kyrgyz Republic and standard mileages and energy consumption figures per vehicle category.

[128] In principle, if financial additionality is proven, the sales level can be higher.

Table 18: Estimated Greenhouse Gas Emissions Reduction Impact per Vehicle Category per Annum for the Kyrgyz Republic

Vehicle Category	Greenhouse Gas Emissions Reduction per Annum (tons of carbon dioxide)
Urban bus	70
Intercity bus	71
Passenger car	3
Taxi	8
Light commercial vehicle for urban deliveries	9
40-ton truck	91

Source: Authors' calculations.

Assuming the target of 1 percentage point growth of EVs for all vehicle categories, by 2030 the EV share would be 5%. A carbon credit program could theoretically generate by 2030 around 1 million tCO_2 reductions with revenues of around $30 million. The recommended approach would be to have a general e-mobility carbon credit program for the country including various EV categories as well as charging infrastructure.

Cycling Infrastructure

The Kyrgyz Republic's NDC includes a modest target of 20 km of additional cycling infrastructure per annum, or 100 km by 2030. Assuming a GHG emissions reduction impact per km of cycle lane of around 200 tCO_2, a 20,000 tCO_2 reduction could be achieved by 2030.[129] While a Gold Standard methodology exists for this type of project, transaction costs, especially with the Gold Standard, are a very large share of the potential revenues from such a project, making it hardly feasible for the carbon market.[130]

Intelligent Traffic Management Systems

The NDC 3.0 estimates that ITMS will reduce GHG emissions by 97,000 tCO_2. However, determination of a baseline and project activity-related emissions reductions are very complex—this is why no approved carbon credit methodology exists for this type of project. Based on experience with similar project types, the probability of an approval of an ITMS methodology and its practical application is limited.

[129] Calculation of the GHG impact of cycling lanes is based on the Green Climate Fund ADB e-mobility funding proposal.
[130] Gold Standard. Lightweight Two and Three Wheeled Personal Transportation.

6.3.6. Mongolia

Mongolia has a net-zero target for 2050. Mongolia's GHG mitigation targets under its NDC 3.0 are a reduction of total GHG emissions of 23% by 2030 and 30.3% by 2035 compared to the BAU scenario. While the NDC 3.0 does not include specific transport measures, national policies explicitly promote the transition to electric public transport. The Vision-2050 Long-Term Development Policy, approved in 2020, includes an objective to "develop a low-carbon, productive, and inclusive green economy and contribute to international efforts to mitigate climate change."[131]

Electric Mobility

As of the end of 2023, Mongolia had around 700 EVs registered among a total of more than 1.1 million vehicles. The Development Bank of Mongolia headed the procurement of 46 electric buses, which demonstrated that electric public transport is viable in Ulaanbaatar's harsh winters with proper infrastructure planning.[132]

A plan released by the Ministry of Road and Transport in September 2023 aims to increase Mongolia's number of EVs to 2,000 by 2026. Specific targets are that 60% of passenger vehicles used by state and local organizations are EVs and that 70% of vehicles used in public transportation, mail delivery, and distribution services are EVs.[133]

To access international carbon markets, Mongolia is for all vehicle categories below the threshold values considered as common practice and can thus potentially register EV projects. Based on the IFIs, Mongolia has a very high carbon grid factor of 1,002 gCO_2/kWh which results in low GHG emission reductions of EVs. Table 19 shows the estimated GHG emissions reduction per annum per vehicle that could be claimed with a carbon market project, based on the carbon grid factor of Mongolia and standard mileages and energy consumption figures per vehicle category.

Table 19: Estimated Greenhouse Gas Emissions Reduction Impact per Vehicle Category per Annum for Mongolia

Vehicle Category	Greenhouse Gas Emissions Reduction per Annum (tons of carbon dioxide)
Urban bus	11
Intercity bus	Negative
Passenger car	0.5
Taxi	Negative
Light commercial vehicle for urban deliveries	3
40-ton truck	Negative

Source: Authors' calculations.

[131] Government of Mongolia. 2020. Vision-2050. Long-Term Development Policy of Mongolia.

[132] Sustainable Banking and Finance Network. 2025. Development Bank of Mongolia's Electric Bus Initiative for Sustainable Urban Mobility.

[133] International Bank for Economic Cooperation. 2024. IBEC Supports the Supply and Sales of Electric Vehicles in Mongolia. News release. 2 April.

Due to the very high carbon grid factor, emissions reductions per vehicle unit are low and in some cases even negative. Fostering e-mobility without reducing the carbon grid factor will only have a very small impact on reducing GHG emissions, so a carbon market program in this area is not a priority.

Railways

Mongolia's Long-Term Development Policy targets railway expansion to 1,174 km by 2025, 1,960 km by 2030, and 4,838 km by 2050 (footnote 131). Its second NDC also included railways for coal transport and a mode shift of road to rail as specific mitigation actions, based on two new lines that started operations in 2023. These lines would no longer be eligible for carbon market projects and form part of the transport mitigation actions within the NDC. Increased freight rail volumes would result in GHG emissions reductions with potential depending on freight type, and additional t-km transported. GHG estimates made in a report for Mongolia show three times lower rail than road emissions for freight transport.[134] However, no international carbon market methodology has been developed yet to support mode shift of any rail systems, excluding HSR. A transport methodology (for freight as well as for passenger transport) would need to be developed first to register a railway project. Such a methodology could be entered under the VCS and subsequently be used by railway projects worldwide.

Public Transport

An emphasis on transitioning public transport to electric and natural gas-powered vehicles, coupled with ambitious infrastructure projects like a BRT, LRT, and cable cars demonstrates Mongolia's commitment to decarbonizing the sector.[135]

Carbon market projects in this area could potentially use the approved UNFCCC methodology ACM0016.[136] The methodology determines whether the proposed project activity is already common practice in the host city; if the city already has a share of 20% or more of public transport trips realized in the same public transport category as the proposed project activity, it is considered common practice and non-eligible as a carbon market project. Public transport categories comprise metro, suburban rail, LRT systems including trams, autonomous-rail rapid transit, BRT, and conventional bus system. In the case of Ulaanbaatar this threshold value would not pose a problem, neither for the BRT nor for cable cars (a specific cable car methodology was developed and used by the cable car system of Medellin in Colombia). The cable car project is only expected to have a very low ridership and as such will not warrant the costs of developing and implementing a carbon market project. The BRT at least for its initial stage is also considered too small to warrant the development of a carbon market project. Projects of this type require in the order of 200 million additional passengers per annum (based on using carbon credits for Article 6.2 of the Paris Agreement or the CORSIA market).

134 ADB. 2022. *Vision 2050: Decarbonizing Transport Emissions of Mongolia.*

135 BRT projects were announced years ago; a new target is to start BRT construction with support from ADB in March 2026; Construction of a first cable car line began in March 2025.

136 One eligibility criterion that would need to be clarified is if the new BRT is an upgrade or a new public transport system.

6.3.7. Pakistan

The NDC 3.0 of September 2025 maintains Pakistan's overall target of a 50% reduction of projected GHG emissions relative to BAU by 2030, of which 15% are unconditional and 35% conditional on international financial support, technology transfer, and capacity-building assistance. For 2035, the target is a 17% unconditional reduction. The National Economic Transformation Plan 2024–2029 provides the overarching development pathway for integrating climate action into Pakistan's economic and social agenda.[137]

The National Electric Vehicle Policy 2025–2030 describes the Government of Pakistan's e-mobility targets: By 2030, 30% of all new vehicles sales will be electric, rising to 50% by 2040, and 100% by 2060, with 2 million EVs projected to be on the roads by 2030. For buses the goal is even more ambitious, with 50% of sales by 2030 and 90% by 2040. In the truck segment 30% of new heavy-duty truck sales are to be electric by 2030, and 90% by 2040. NDC 3.0 acknowledges that the target of 30% of EV sales has shown limited progress—as of 2025, around only 53,000 EVs were circulating, mostly motorcycles. NDC 3.0 includes as a priority mitigation target that 30% of vehicle sales are electric and that 3,000 chargers operate in the country. Additional transport measures in the NDC are to expand mass transit in major cities, modernize railways to increase the freight share from road to rail, and encourage research and development in green hydrogen. These targets are not separated into unconditional and conditional.

The National Electric Vehicle Policy offers subsidies for electric two-wheelers, three-wheelers, and four-wheelers. It also includes other incentives such as zero registration tolls and tax exemptions and customs duties reductions for local EV manufacturers.

Electric Mobility

As mentioned, the government is targeting 30% of vehicle sales being electric by 2030 or around 2 million EVs operating. In 2018, Pakistan had 24 million vehicles registered, comprising 17.5 million motorcycles, 3 million cars, 0.3 million trucks, and 0.25 million buses. Estimates for 2025 indicate that the country now has 40 million motorcycles, with estimated sales of 2.5 million per year.[138]

To access international carbon markets Pakistan is for all vehicle categories below the threshold values considered as common practice and can thus potentially register EV projects. Based on the IFIs, Pakistan has a carbon grid factor of 386 gCO_2/kWh, which is close to the global average. Table 20 shows estimated GHG emissions reduction per annum per vehicle that could be claimed through a carbon market project, based on the carbon grid factor of Pakistan and standard mileages and energy consumption figures per vehicle category.

[137] Government of Pakistan, Ministry of Planning,Development & Special Initiatives. 2024. *National Economic Transformation Plan 2024-2029*.
[138] Top 10 countries with the highest motorcycle usage.

Table 20: Estimated GHG Emissions Reduction Impact per Vehicle Category per Annum for Pakistan

Vehicle Category	Greenhouse Gas Emissions Reduction per Annum (tons of carbon dioxide)
Urban bus	51
Intercity bus	22
Passenger car	3
Taxi	5
Light commercial vehicle for urban deliveries	8
40-ton truck	49
Motorcycle (commercial unit)	0.8

Source: Authors' calculations.

Assuming a constant share of vehicles per category and the target of 2 million EVs by 2030, a carbon credit project could capture emissions reductions of close to 5 million tCO_2 by 2030, with a corresponding revenue potential of $150 million. The recommended approach would be to have a general e-mobility carbon credit program for the country, including various EV categories as well as charging infrastructure.

Mass Transit Projects

With ADB assistance, Pakistan is implementing mass transit projects in multiple cities, primarily BRT. Carbon market projects in this area could use the approved UNFCCC methodology ACM0016, which determines whether a proposed project activity is common practice in the city for which it is proposed. If the city already has a share of 20% or more of public transport trips realized on the same public transport category as the proposed project activity, it is considered as common practice and non-eligible as carbon market project. Public transport categories include metro, suburban rail, LRT including trams, autonomous-rail rapid transit, BRT, and conventional bus system. Most cities in Pakistan could apply, e.g., with BRT systems. While e-mobility projects can be grouped well, this is less the case with mass transit projects as the baseline and monitoring system is unique for each city. Therefore, carbon credit projects in this area are formulated as standalone projects. Karachi's BRT, for instance, would reduce around 70,000 tCO_2 per annum (for mode shift portion only, i.e., excluding shifting to biogas or electric buses). However, such projects are complex to develop and monitor and require at this size prices of at least $15/$tCO_2$ to warrant realization.

Rail Projects

Pakistan intends to increase the rail share of its freight transport. Increased freight rail volumes would result in GHG emissions reductions, with the magnitude depending on the freight type, and additional t-km transported. However, no international carbon market methodology has been developed yet to support mode shift of any rail systems, excluding HSR. A transport methodology (for freight as well as for passenger transport) would need to be developed first to register a railway project. Such a methodology could be entered under the VCS and subsequently be used by railway projects worldwide.

6.3.8. Tajikistan

Tajikistan's NDC promotes e-mobility as one of its core mitigation actions within the transport sector. Dushanbe authorities plan to achieve a full transition to electric public transport by 2028. Part of that goal is to replace 500 currently operating buses with battery electric buses. Dushanbe-based taxi companies are mandated to completely shift to electric taxis by September 2025. This initiative began in 2021 and by mid-2024, the city had more than 100 charging stations and around 2,500 EVs among its 4,400 taxis.

To access international carbon markets Tajikistan is for all vehicle categories below the threshold values considered as common practice and can thus potentially register EV projects. Taxis in Dushanbe would however not be eligible as the shift to EVs has been declared compulsory—if EVs are compulsory, this is the baseline and such a project would not be additional.[139]

Based on the IFIs, the country has a low carbon grid factor of 106 gCO_2/kWh. Table 21 shows the estimated GHG emissions reduction per annum per vehicle that could be claimed with a carbon market project, based on the carbon grid factor of Tajikistan and standard mileages and energy consumption figures per vehicle category.

Table 21: Estimated GHG Emissions Reduction Impact per Vehicle Category per Annum for Tajikistan

Vehicle Category	Greenhouse Gas Emissions Reduction per Annum (tons of carbon dioxide)
Urban bus	69
Intercity bus	70
Passenger car	4
Taxi	8
Light commercial vehicle for urban deliveries	10
40-ton truck	90

Source: Authors' calculations.

The 5,000 electric taxis thus reduce around 40,000 tCO_2 per annum; however, as mentioned, this would not be an eligible carbon market project. The 500 proposed urban electric buses for Dushanbe would reduce annually around 35,000 tCO_2 and this project would be eligible, potentially generating additional annual climate finance worth close to $1 million. However, it would be more efficient to make a general e-mobility carbon credit program for all EV types including charging infrastructure, thereby reaching much higher volumes, incorporating smaller companies, and allowing for reduced transaction costs per ton of carbon issued as credit.

[139] The setting of EV targets is compatible with carbon market projects, but not compulsory deployment of EVs.

6.3.9. Turkmenistan

Turkmenistan's NDC targeted areas for GHG emissions mitigation in the transport sector include the promotion of public transport and a transition to cleaner and more economical fuels such as CNG or liquefied petroleum gas. In Arkadag City, a newly constructed city opened in 2023, public transport is predominantly based on electric buses and taxis. However, there are no published policies or targets to promote EVs. Shifting toward gaseous fuels in the transport sector will only have a marginal GHG impact, if at all, due to high energy usage of gas-powered vehicles and methane slip emissions at different stages of gas usage (e.g., vehicle, fueling). Turkmenistan has a relatively high carbon grid factor of 676 gCO_2/kWh, which still results in GHG emissions reductions of EVs but at a minor scale compared to other countries (Table 22).

Table 22: Estimated GHG Emissions Reduction Impact per Vehicle Category per Annum for Turkmenistan

Vehicle Category	Greenhouse Gas Emissions Reduction per Annum (tons of carbon dioxide)
Urban bus	32
Intercity bus	No reduction
Passenger car	1.5
Taxi	2
Light commercial vehicle for urban deliveries	6
40-ton truck	8

Source: Authors' calculations.

Turkmenistan is also studying the gradual transition of railway transport to electric traction, alongside reducing empty runs and ensuring efficient loading. Shifting to electric traction is not expected to have a large impact on GHG emissions reduction due to Turkmenistan's high carbon grid factor and the high efficiency of diesel locos. Increasing efficiency in rail systems is very difficult to structure as a carbon market project due to methodological difficulties in establishing a credible baseline.

Increased promotion and usage of public transport and the involved mode shift could presumably fit best for a carbon market project. However, this would require investments in new mass transit systems and not just efficiency improvements to be eligible under existing carbon market methodologies for public transit.

6.3.10. Uzbekistan

Under Uzbekistan's NDC 3.0, no specific transport targets are mentioned although transport mitigation measures mentioned are the electrification of railways, the fostering of public transport, and the transition to environmentally friendly transport. Electrification of the transport sector is considered a key measure. An initial focus is thereby on the public transport fleet. Uzbekistan promotes electric transport and aims to convert 80% of public transport to gas and electricity by 2030. The government also provides fiscal incentives for EVs.

Electric Mobility

Uzbekistan imported around 26,000 EVs in 2023 and strongly promotes electric buses. By 2030, Uzbekistan intends to expand its overall bus fleet to 5,000 units, including 2,000 electric buses.[140] In 2023, the country bought its first 1,000 e-buses. As of 2025, Tashkent operated over 300 electric buses; 200 additional e-buses shall enter the fleet in October 2025, and an additional 1,000 units in 2026.[141] As of 2025, Samarkand had 100 e-buses in operation and plans to receive an additional 330.

To access international carbon markets Uzbekistan is for all vehicle categories below the threshold values considered as common practice. Based on the IFIs, the country has an average carbon grid factor of 467 gCO_2/kWh. Table 23 shows the estimated GHG emissions reduction per annum per vehicle which could be claimed with a carbon market project, based on the carbon grid factor of Uzbekistan and standard mileages and energy consumption figures per vehicle category.

The already purchased and operational e-buses are no longer eligible for a carbon market program. New units, however, would be eligible. An additional 1,000 electric buses reduce around 46,000 tCO_2 per annum and could generate climate finance worth close to $1 million.

Table 23: Estimated Greenhouse Gas Emissions Reduction Impact per Vehicle Category per Annum for Uzbekistan

Vehicle Category	Greenhouse Gas Emissions Reduction Per Annum (tons of carbon dioxide)
Urban bus	46
Intercity bus	22
Passenger car	2.5
Taxi	4
Light commercial vehicle for urban deliveries	7
40-ton truck	38

Source: Authors' calculations.

[140] Asian Transport Outlook . 2024. *Transport and Climate Profile: Uzbekistan*; and Government of the Republic of Uzbekistan. 2021. *Updated Nationally Determined Contribution*.

[141] M. Sultanova. 2025. Uzbekistan to Expand Tashkent's Fleet with 1,200 New Electric and Modern Buses by 2026. *Daryo*. 9 October.

However, it would be more efficient to make a general e-mobility carbon credit program for all EV types, including charging infrastructure, thereby reaching much higher volumes, incorporating smaller companies, and allowing for reduced transaction costs per ton of carbon issued as credit.

6.3.11. Summary of Potential Pipeline Carbon Market Transport Projects

Most countries aim to reduce GHG transport emissions through electric mobility, public transport, and rail mode shift. Other activities such as fostering NMT, efficiency improvements, intelligent transport systems, or gaseous fuels are less relevant for carbon markets due to their limited size, difficulties establishing a credible baseline, or a questionable GHG impact. Table 24 shows the project types that match well with potential carbon market projects by country.

Table 24: Matching Priority Areas with Carbon Market Projects per Country

Country	Electric Mobility	Public Transport	Rail Projects
Azerbaijan	Feasible	Feasible	
China, People's Republic of		Feasible	Partially feasible
Georgia	Feasible	Partially feasible	
Kazakhstan	Feasible		Feasible
Kyrgyz Republic	Feasible		
Mongolia		Partially feasible	Feasible
Pakistan	Feasible	Feasible	Feasible
Tajikistan	Feasible		
Turkmenistan	Partially feasible	Partially feasible	
Uzbekistan	Feasible	Feasible	Feasible

[green] = Feasible for carbon markets and national priority, [orange] = Partially feasible for carbon markets.
Source: Authors' assessments.

Electric mobility is a priority in many countries for decarbonizing the transport sector and lends itself well to carbon market projects. Limitations occur in countries where usage or deployment of certain EV types (e.g., taxis or urban buses) are mandated by law or where they are included as an unconditional commitment under an NDC. Another limiting factor is that carbon market methodologies in this area have threshold values expressed as sales percentages of EVs (under the EV CDM and VCS methodologies, the sales share of EVs of their respective vehicle category needs to be below 2.5% as average for the last 3 years) and as market share (in terms of vehicle stock) of EVs per vehicle category to be still considered as additional and not as BAU. These tipping points have been surpassed in the case of the PRC for most vehicle categories, and while this is not so for other countries, the situation can change very fast as the experience of Nepal and Thailand shows. The window of opportunity to register carbon market projects for e-mobility is closing fast.

Public transport projects are also a common priority in many CAREC countries and are suited to carbon markets due to them having approved methodologies. Mass transit methodologies also include tipping points to separate additional from BAU projects. However, these are defined for each mass transit project type and do not create a problem for most cities and countries. The critical issue for such projects is that they need to be based on new infrastructure, not just new rolling stock or vehicles, and require many additional passengers to warrant the high development and monitoring costs of such projects. In contrast to e-mobility projects, a grouping of such projects also makes limited or no sense as baseline and monitoring are unique to each city and transport system. Another limitation of such projects is their long gestation period and in general an overestimation of ridership in the planning phase, resulting in lower-than-expected emissions reductions during implementation. As of 2025, pure efficiency improvement projects in public transport were not eligible under existing methodologies and developing an acceptable methodology in this area is very demanding due to difficult baseline determination.

Rail projects are also popular among CAREC countries, especially for freight transport. Infrastructure expansion would be potentially eligible for carbon market projects. However, outside HSR, no approved and usable methodology exists to determine the GHG emissions reduction impact of such projects within carbon markets. Such a methodology would need to be developed separately for freight and passenger transport. Some indents have been made, albeit without success (outside domestic markets, which only require national or provincial approvals). Developing a new carbon market methodology is a lengthy and costly procedure and methodologies are thereafter public goods. This reduces the incentive for private project developers to develop them. Rail infrastructure projects need to be a considerable size in terms of additional t-km and/or passenger-km transported to warrant development and monitoring costs. Some countries have proposed initiatives such as efficiency improvements or electrification of rail systems but again, no approved and widely used methodologies exist. Electrification would be relatively straightforward to develop as a methodology, but the resulting emissions reductions are in general limited. Efficiency improvements are extremely difficult to account for in carbon markets due to difficulties in determining a credible baseline or BAU development.

www.ingramcontent.com/pod-product-compliance
Lightning Source LLC
Chambersburg PA
CBHW041757220926
51847CB00014B/234